PETERSON   BAKER   BAVIER   WILLIAMS   DAVIE

Edge Cloud Operations

A Systems Approach

SYSTEMS APPROACH LLC

Contents

Foreword

First the applications all moved to the cloud. And now they're being torn apart. Let me explain what I mean by that.

As markets grow, the unit of function around which one can build a business shrinks. A classic example of this can be seen in the history of the automotive industry. The Ford River Rouge Complex was built in the late 1920s. At the time, mass-produced cars were relatively new, and the market was relatively small. And so factories like the River Rouge Complex had to build all the subcomponents too. Roughly, in one side of the factory went water, rubber, and iron ore, and out the other side came full automobiles. Of course, as the market for cars grew, so did a massive ecosystem of suppliers of car components: wheels, seats, floor mats, and the like. Today the large car companies are more akin to integrators than auto parts makers.

The same dynamic is happening with the application. In the 1970s the same manufacturer would build the chips, the circuit boards, the system form factor, the operating system, and each of the applications. Over time as the market has grown, the system has disaggregated. The hardware and software separated and spawned multiple independent companies. And then companies started to be built around independent applications.

The market hasn't stopped growing and over the last few years we've seen the application itself disaggregate. Commonly used subcomponents of applications are being pulled out, and entire companies and projects are being built around them. Today, if you're building an application, there are third-party APIs available for authenticating users, sending texts or email, streaming videos, authorizing access to resources, and many other useful functions.

So what does this have to do with the book you're about to read? While the last decade was a consolidation of applications into the cloud, the next decade is largely going to be about the explosion of applications and application components away from it. Now that sub-components of workloads have been largely decoupled from having to sit with the application, they can be run anywhere. And in particular they can be run on infrastructure that's purposely built and optimized for them! In fact, we are starting to see what can only be described as an anti-cloud trend where large companies are choosing to pull some workloads back from large clouds to their own optimized infras-tructure. And we're even seeing startups choosing to build their own infrastructure from the get-go because they understand the cost and performance advantages of doing so.

In "Edge Cloud Operations: A Systems Approach" the authors provide a detailed overview of not just cloud operations (which are so last decade) but operations in this new era of distributed clouds. In many ways, the cloud era was a low point of systems, because so much below the application layer was buried deep within the engi-neering organizations of the three large cloud providers. But that's changing, and to change with it, you need to understand how it all works. And that's exactly why you need to read this book.

Martin Casado
General Partner, a16z

Preface

The cloud is ubiquitous. Everyone uses the cloud to either access or deliver services, but not everyone will build and operate a cloud. So why should anyone care about how to turn a pile of servers and switches into a 24/7 service delivery platform? That's what Google, Microsoft, Amazon and the other cloud providers do for us, and they do a perfectly good job of it.

The answer, we believe, is that the cloud is becoming ubiquitous in another way, as distributed applications increasingly run not just in large, central datacenters but at the edge. As applications are disaggregated, the cloud is expanding from hundreds of datacenters to tens of thousands of enterprises. And while it is clear that the commodity cloud providers are eager to manage those edge clouds as a logical extension of their datacenters, they do not have a monopoly on the know-how for making that happen.

At the same time edge applications are moving to the forefront, increasing importance is also being placed on *digital sovereignty*, the ability of countries and organizations to control their destiny and their data. Cloud technology is important for running today's workloads, but access to that technology does not necessarily have to be bundled with outsourcing operational control.

This book lays out a roadmap that a small team of engineers followed over the course of a year to stand up and operationalize an edge cloud and then operate it 24/7. This edge cloud spans a dozen enterprises, and hosts a non-trivial cloud native service—5G connectivity in our case, but that's just an example. The team was able to do this by leveraging 20+ open source components, but selecting those components is just a start. There were dozens of technical decisions to make along the way, and a few thousand lines of configuration code to write. We believe this is a repeatable exercise, which we report in this book. The code for those configuration files is open source, for those who want to pursue the topic in more detail.

What do we mean by an edge cloud? We're drawing a distinction between clouds run by the hyperscale cloud providers in their massive data centers, which we think of as the core, and those run by enterprises (or managed for them) at the edge. The edge is where the real, physical world meets the cloud. For example, it is the place where data from sensors is likely to be gathered and processed, and where services that need to be close to the end user for reasons of latency or bandwidth are delivered.

Our roadmap may not be the right one for all circumstances, but it does shine a light on the fundamental challenges and trade-offs involved in operationalizing a cloud. As we can attest based on our experience, it's a complicated design space with an overabundance of terminology and storylines to untangle.

Intended Audience

We hope this book makes valuable reading for anyone who is trying to stand up and operationalize their own edge cloud infrastructure, but we also aim to provide useful information for at least two other broad groups.

First, there will be a set of readers who need to evaluate the options available, particularly to decide between using the cloud services offered by one of the hyperscalers or building their own edge cloud (or some combination of these). We hope to demystify the landscape of edge clouds for this audience to help inform those decisions.

Secondly, there will be a group of application and service developers who need to build on top of whatever cloud infrastructure their organization has chosen to use. We believe it is important for these developers to understand what goes on "under the hood" of the cloud at least at a high level, so that they can make their applications manageable and reliable. There is increasingly close interaction between developers and operators (as evidenced by the DevOps movement) and we aim to facilitate that collaboration. Topics such as monitoring and observability are particularly important for this audience.

Guided Tour of Open Source

The good news is that there is a wealth of open source components that can be assembled to help manage cloud platforms and scalable applications built on those platforms. That's also the bad news. With several dozen cloud-related projects available at open source consortia such as the Linux Foundation, Cloud Native Computing Foundation, and Apache Foundation, navigating the project space is one of the biggest challenges we faced in putting together a cloud management platform. This is in large part because these projects are competing for mindshare, with both significant overlap in the functionality they offer and dependencies on each other.

One way to read this book is as a guided tour of the open source landscape for cloud control and management. And in that spirit, we do not replicate the excellent documentation those projects already provide, but instead include links to project-specific documentation (which often includes tutorials that we encourage you to try). We also include snippets of code from those projects, but these examples are chosen to help solidify the main points we're trying to make about the management platform as a whole; they should not be interpreted as an attempt to document the inner working of the individual projects. Our goal is to explain how the various puzzle pieces fit together to build an end-to-end management system, and in doing so, identify both various tools that help and the hard problems that no amount of tooling can eliminate.

It should come as no surprise that there are challenging technical issues to address (despite marketing claims to the contrary). After all, how to operationalize a computing system is a question that's as old as the field of *Operating Systems*. Operationalizing a cloud is just today's version of that fundamental problem, which has become all the more interesting as we move up the stack, from managing *devices* to managing *services*. This topic is both timely and foundational.

Acknowledgements

Aether, the example edge cloud this book uses to illustrate how to operationalize a cloud, was built by the Open Networking Foundation (ONF) engineering team and the open source community that worked with them. We acknowledge their contributions, with a special thank-you to Hyunsun Moon, Sean Condon, and HungWei Chiu for their significant contributions to Aether's control and management platform, and to Oguz Sunay for his influence on Aether's overall design. Suchitra Vemuri's insights into testing and quality assurance were also invaluable.

The ONF is no longer active, but Aether continues as an open source project of the Linux Foundation. Visit `https://aetherproject.org` to learn about the ongoing project. We will also happily accept feedback to this book. Please send us your comments using the Issues Link, or submit a Pull Request with suggested changes.

Larry Peterson, Scott Baker, Andy Bavier, Zack Williams, and Bruce Davie

June 2025

Chapter 1: Introduction

Clouds provide a set of tools for bringing up and operating scalable services, but how do you operationalize a cloud in the first place? The two problems are not mutually exclusive—after all, a cloud is realized as a set of services—but asking the question this way eliminates the temptation to give the answer "the cloud takes care of that for you." This book describes how to operationalize a cloud, starting with bare-metal hardware, all the way to offering one or more managed services.

Few of us are likely to have reason to instantiate a hyperscale datacenter, but deploying private edge clouds in an enterprise—and optionally connecting that edge to a datacenter to form a hybrid cloud—is becoming increasingly common. We use the term "edge cloud" to distinguish our focus from the "core", which is the traditional domain of the hyperscale operators. The edge is more likely to be in a enterprise or an "Internet of Things" setting such as a factory. The edge is the place where the cloud services connect to the real world, e.g., via sensors and actuators, and where latency-sensitive services are deployed to be close to the consumers of those services.[1]

The hyperscalers are indeed willing to manage your edge cloud for you, as an extension of their core datacenters. And correspondingly, there is significant activity to provide such products, with Google's Anthos, Microsoft's Azure Arc, and Amazon's ECS-Anywhere as prime examples. But the barrier to operationalizing a cloud is not so high that only a hyperscaler has the wherewithal to do it. It is possible to build a cloud—and all the associated lifecycle management and runtime controls that are required to operate it—using readily available open source software packages.

[1] Server clusters hosted in co-location facilities can also be considered edge clouds, and benefit from the technologies and practices described in this book, but we use enterprises as our exemplar deployment because they expose a broader set of requirements.

This book describes what such a cloud management platform looks like. Our approach is to focus on the fundamental problems that must be addressed—design issues that are common to all clouds—but then couple this conceptual discussion with specific engineering choices made while operationalizing a specific enterprise cloud. Our example is Aether, an open source edge cloud that supports 5G connectivity as a managed service. Aether has the following properties that make it an interesting use case to study:

- Aether starts with bare-metal hardware (servers and switches) deployed in edge sites (e.g., enterprises). This on-prem cloud can range in size from a partial rack to multi-rack cluster, assembled according to the best practices used in datacenters.

- Aether supports both "edge services" running on these on-prem clusters and "centralized services" running in commodity cloud datacenters. In this sense it is a hybrid cloud.[2]

- Aether augments this edge cloud with 5G-Connectivity-as-a-Service, giving us a service that must be operationalized (in addition to the underlying cloud). The end result is that Aether provides a managed Platform-as-a-Service (PaaS).

- Aether is built entirely from open source components. The only thing it adds is the "glue code" and "specification directives" required to make it operational. This means the recipe is fully reproducible by anyone that follows the linked documentation.

There is another important reason Aether makes for an interesting example. It is a system being deployed at the confluence of three traditionally distinct management domains: enterprises (where system admins have long been responsible for installing and maintaining purpose-built appliances), network operators (where access technologies have historically been delivered as Telco-based solutions), and cloud providers (where commodity hardware and cloud native software is now readily available). This complicates our job, because each of these three domains brings its own conventions and terminology to the table. But understanding how these three stakeholders approach

[2] Technically, Aether is also a multi-cloud because it is designed to take advantage of services provided by multiple public clouds, but the private/public (edge/central) aspect is the most relevant, so we use hybrid terminology throughout this book.

Further Reading:
Aether: 5G-Connected Edge Cloud (`https://opennetworking.org/aether/`).

Aether Documentation (`https://docs.aetherproject.org/master/index.html`).

operationalization gives us a broader perspective on the problem. We return to the confluence of enterprise, cloud, and access technologies later in this chapter, but we start by addressing the terminology challenge.

> **Developers Have an Equal Role to Play**
>
> *This book takes an operator-centric view of cloud operations, but developers have an equal role to play. This role is reflected in practices like DevOps (which we discuss in Section 2.5), but can also been seen in the underlying system design. The cloud architecture includes a management platform, which specifies a runtime interface through which service developers (who provide functionality) interact with cloud operators (who manage that functionality). Because there is a shared management platform to leverage, developers do not need to (and should not) reinvent the wheel when it comes to provisioning, configuring, controlling, and monitoring the services they implement.*
>
> *Looking at the broader picture, this management platform is an essential part of how app builders and service developers deliver functionality to end users. Today, functionality is most often delivered as a Managed Service (as opposed to an inert pile of software). This means developers not only have to worry about the algorithms and data structures needed to implement their app or service, they also need to interface with the platform that operationalizes (activates) their code. It is common to focus on the former and view the latter as a burden (especially if someone else will be responsible for deploying and operating their code), but coding to the management platform interface is a central part of the contract for delivering a managed service. Understanding and appreciating the "hows" and "whys" of this platform is critical to developers doing their job.*

1.1 Terminology

The terminology used to talk about operating cloud services represents a mix of "modern" concepts that are native to the cloud, and "traditional" concepts that are artifacts from earlier systems (many of which are now being subsumed by the cloud, but retain some of their original operational language). This is especially true at the intersection of the cloud and Telcos, who—like the Sámi of Scandinavia having over 180 words for snow—have an exceedingly rich vocabulary for *operating* a network.

A major source of confusion is that we are in the midst of a transition from network systems being built from purpose-built *devices* to software-based *services* running on commodity hardware. This often results in multiple terms being used for the same concept, or more problematically, having one domain subtly repurpose a term from another domain. To avoid talking past each other, it is important to first define a few concepts and introduce the related terminology.

- **Operations & Maintenance (O&M):** A traditional term used to characterize the overall challenge of operationalizing a network, where generally speaking, operators use an O&M Interface to manage the system.

  - **FCAPS:** An acronym (Fault, Configuration, Accounting, Performance, Security) historically used in the Telco industry to enumerate the requirements for an operational system. The O&M interface must provide a means to detect and manage faults, configure the system, account for usage, and so on.

  - **OSS/BSS:** Another Telco acronym (Operations Support System, Business Support System), referring to the subsystem that implements both operational logic (OSS) and business logic (BSS). It is usually the top-most component in the overall O&M hierarchy.

  - **EMS:** Yet another Telco acronym (Element Management System), corresponding to an intermediate layer in the overall O&M hierarchy. An EMS is to a particular type of device what an OSS/BSS is to the network as a whole.

- **Orchestration:** A general term similar to O&M, but originating in the cloud context. Involves assembling (e.g., allocating, configuring, connecting) a collection of physical or logical resources on behalf of some workload. If only a single resource or device is involved, we would probably use a term like "configuration" instead, so orchestration typically implies "orchestrating" across multiple components.

Narrowly defined, an orchestrator is responsible for spinning up virtual machines (or containers) and logically interconnecting them (with virtual networks). More broadly, orchestration encompasses aspects of all the management-related functions described in this book.

If you are trying to map cloud terminology onto Telco terminology, an orchestrator is often equated with a cloudified version of the OSS/BSS mechanism. This top-most layer is sometimes called a *Service Orchestrator* since it is responsible for assembling a collection of *Virtual Network Functions (VNFs)* into an end-to-end-service chain.

- **Playbook/Workflow:** A program or script that implements a multi-step orchestration process. (The term workflow is also used in a UX context to describe a multi-step operation that a user performs on a system using a GUI.)

• **Provisioning:** Adding capacity (either physical or virtual resources) to a system, usually in response to changes in workload, including the initial deployment.

- **Zero-Touch Provisioning:** Usually implies adding new hardware without requiring a human to configure it (beyond physically connecting the device). This implies the new component auto-configures itself, which means the term can also be applied to virtual resources (e.g., virtual machines, services) to indicate that no manual configuration step is needed to instantiate the resource.

- **Remote Device Management:** A standard (e.g., IPMI, Redfish) that defines a way to remotely manage hardware devices in support of zero-touch provisioning. The idea is to send and receive out-of-band messages over the LAN in place of having video or serial console access to the device. Additionally, these may integrate with monitoring and other device health telemetry systems.

    – **Inventory Management:** Planning and tracking both the physical (racks, servers, switches, cabling) and virtual (IP ranges and addresses, VLANs) resources is a sub-step of the provisioning process. This process frequently starts using simple spreadsheets and text files, but as complexity grows, a dedicated database for inventory facilitates greater automation.

- **Lifecycle Management:** Upgrading and replacing functionality (e.g., new services, new features to existing services) over time.

    – **Continuous Integration / Continuous Deployment (CI/CD):** An approach to Lifecycle Management in which the path from development (producing new functionality) to testing, integration, and ultimately deployment is an automated pipeline. CI/CD typically implies continuously making small incremental changes rather than performing large disruptive upgrades.

    – **DevOps:** An engineering discipline that fuses the Development process and Operational requirements silos, balancing feature velocity against system reliability. As a practice, it leverages CI/CD methods and is typically associated with container-based (also known as *cloud native*) systems. There is some overlap between DevOps and *Site Reliability Engineering (SRE)* as practiced by cloud providers such as Google.

    – **In-Service Software Upgrade (ISSU):** A requirement that a component continue running during the deployment of an upgrade, with minimal disruption to the service delivered to end-users. ISSU generally implies the ability to incrementally roll-out (and roll-back) an upgrade, but is specifically a requirement on individual components (as opposed to the platform used to manage a set of components).

- **Monitoring & Telemetry:** Collecting data from system components to aid in management decisions. This includes diagnosing faults, tuning performance, doing root cause analysis, performing security audits, and provisioning additional capacity.

    – **Analytics:** A program (often using statistical models) that produces additional insights (value) from raw data. It can be used to close a control loop (i.e., auto-reconfigure a system based on these insights), but could also be targeted at a human operator who subsequently takes some action.

Another way to talk about operations is in terms of stages, leading to a characterization that is common for traditional network devices:

- **Day (-1):** Hardware configuration that is applied to a device (e.g., via a console) when it is first powered on. These configurations correspond to firmware (BIOS or similar) settings, and often need knowledge of how the device is physically connected to the network (e.g., the port being used).

- **Day 0:** Connectivity configuration required to establish communication between the device and the available network services (e.g., setting a device's IP address and default router). While such information may be provided manually, this is an opportunity to auto-configure the device, in support of Zero-Touch Provisioning.

- **Day 1:** Service-level configuration needed by the device, including parameters that allow the device to take advantage of other services (e.g., NTP, Syslog, SMTP, NFS), as well as setting the parameters this device needs to perform whatever service it provides. At the end of Day-1 operationalization, the device is considered up-and-running, and able to support user traffic. This is also an opportunity for zero-touch provisioning, in the sense that pre-programmed playbooks (workflows) should be able to auto-configure the device rather than depending on human intervention.

- **Day 2..N:** On-going management in support of day-to-day operations, coupled with monitoring the network to detect failures and service degradation, with the goal of sustaining the service. This may involve some closed-loop control, but is often human-intense, which involves monitoring a dashboard and fielding alerts, and then re-configuring the system as necessary. This is often referred to simply as "Day 2 Operations".

Again, "Day x" is how traditional network vendors characterize the process of operationalizing the devices they sell, which in turn dictates how network operators and enterprise system admins bring those devices online. While the general framework has been extended to Virtual Network Functions (VNFs), it is still a device-centric view of operations. But once a system becomes cloud native, two things shift the balance of concerns. First, all hardware is commodity, and so Days 0 and 1 configurations become fully automated (and Day -1 is minimized since all devices are identical).[3] Second, Day 2 operations become a much more sophisticated process. This is because software-based systems are more agile, making functional upgrades more commonplace. This focus on *feature velocity* is one of the inherent values of cloud-based systems, but not surprisingly, it brings its own set of challenges to management.

This book addresses those management challenges, which brings us to a final note about two words we use frequently: *Operating* and *Operationalizing*. Being able to operate a cloud is the end goal and implies an ongoing process, whereas to operationalize a cloud implies the process of bringing a set of hardware and software components into a state that makes it easy to sustain their ongoing operation. This distinction is relevant because operationalizing a cloud is not a one-time proposition, but rather, an essential aspect of day-to-day operations. Being rapidly evolvable is one of the cloud's most important features, making continual operationalization a key requirement for operating an edge cloud.

1.2 Disaggregation

To fully understand the challenge of operating a cloud, we have to start with the underlying building blocks: a collection of software-based microservices running on commodity hardware. These building blocks are the consequence of having *disaggregated* the bundled and purpose-built network appliances that came before. From the management perspective, it is helpful to identify what becomes easier and what becomes harder when you make this transition. This is both the challenge and the opportunity of disaggregation.

Broadly speaking, disaggregation is the process of breaking large bundled components into a set of smaller constituent parts. SDN is

[3] Colloquially, this is sometimes referred to as a shift from taking care of pets to one of herding cattle.

one example of disaggregation—it decouples the network's control and data planes, with the former running as a cloud service and the latter running in commodity switches. The microservice architecture is another example of disaggregation—it breaks monolithic cloud applications into a mesh of single-function components. Disaggregation is widely viewed as an essential step in accelerating feature velocity. This is the opportunity side of the story, which is one of the widely-claimed benefits of cloud native application architectures. A useful, if opinionated, view of such architectures is the Twelve-Factor App.

The challenge side of the story is that there are many more moving parts that have to be integrated, coordinated, and managed. Circling back to terminology, Orchestration and Lifecycle Management become the dominant issues because (a) many smaller parts have to be assembled, and (b) these individual parts are expected to change more frequently. Much of this book focuses on these two issues.

The good news is that the industry seems to have converged on *containers* as the common representation for "component packaging" and Kubernetes as the first-level *container orchestrator*. (We say "first-level" because Kubernetes is not sufficient by itself.) This foundation, in turn, makes many of the other challenges more manageable:

- Monitoring and other telemetry-related mechanisms are themselves realized as a set of container-based microservices, deployed within the cloud they observe.

- ISSU becomes more tractable because the microservice architecture encourages stateless components, with persistent state isolated in a single function-agnostic storage service, such as a key-value store.

- Zero-Touch Provisioning is more tractable because the hardware is commodity, and hence, (nearly) identical. This also means the vast majority of configuration involves initializing software parameters, which is more readily automated.

- Cloud native implies a set of best practices for addressing many of the FCAPS requirements, especially as they relate to availability and performance, both of which are achieved through horizontal

Further Reading:
Adam Wiggins. The Twelve-Factor App (`https://12factor.net/`).

scaling. Secure communication is also typically built into cloud
RPC mechanisms.

Another way to say this is that by rearchitecting bundled appliances
and devices as horizontally scalable microservices running on commodity hardware, what used to be a set of one-off O&M problems are
now solved by widely applied best practices from distributed systems,
which have in turn been codified in state-of-the-art cloud management
frameworks (like Kubernetes). This leaves us with the problem of (a)
provisioning commodity hardware, (b) orchestrating the container
building blocks, (c) deploying microservices to collect and archive
monitoring data in a uniform way, and (d) continually integrating and
deploying individual microservices as they evolve over time.

Finally, because a cloud is infinitely programmable, the system
being managed has the potential to change substantially over time.[4]
This means that the cloud management system must itself be easily
extended to support new features (as well as the refactoring of existing features). This is accomplished in part by implementing the cloud
management system as a cloud service, which means we will see a fair
amount of recursive dependencies throughout this book. It also points
to taking advantage of declarative specifications of how all the disaggregated pieces fit together. These specifications can then be used
to generate elements of the management system, rather than having
to manually recode them. This is a subtle issue we will return to in
later chapters, but ultimately, we want to be able to auto-configure the
subsystem responsible for auto-configuring the rest of the system.

[4] For example, compare the two services Amazon offered ten years ago (EC2 and S3) with the well over 100 services available on the AWS console today (not counting the marketplace of partner-provided services).

1.3 Cloud Technology

Being able to operationalize a cloud starts with the building blocks
used to construct the cloud in the first place. This section summarizes
the available technology, with the goal of identifying the baseline capabilities of the underlying system. This baseline is then assumed by
the collection of management-related subsystems described throughout this book.

Before identifying these building blocks, we need to acknowledge that we are venturing into a gray area, having to do with what you consider to be "part of the platform being managed" versus "part of the subsystem that manages the platform." To further complicate matters, where you draw the line shifts over time as technology matures and becomes ubiquitous.

For example, if you start with the premise that a cloud hosts a set of containers, then your management layer would be responsible for detecting and restarting failed containers. On the other hand, if you assume containers are resilient (i.e., able to auto-recover), then the management layer would not need to include that functionality (although it probably still needs to detect when the auto-recovery mechanism fails and correct for that). This is not a unique situation—complex systems often include mechanisms that address problems at multiple levels. For the purpose of this book, we just need to decide on a line that separates "technology that is assumed" from "problems that remain and how we address them." The following identifies the technology we assume.

1.3.1 Hardware Platform

The assumed hardware building blocks are straightforward. We start with bare-metal servers and switches, built using merchant silicon chips. These might, for example, be ARM or x86 processor chips and Tomahawk or Tofino switching chips, respectively. The bare-metal boxes also include a bootstrap mechanism (e.g., BIOS for servers and ONIE for switches), and a remote device management interface (e.g., IPMI or Redfish).

Further Reading:
Redfish (`https://www.dmtf.org/standards/redfish`).

A physical cloud cluster is then constructed with the hardware building blocks arranged as shown in Figure 1: one or more racks of servers connected by a leaf-spine switching fabric. The servers are shown above the switching fabric to emphasize that software running on the servers controls the switches.

Figure 1 also includes the assumed low-level software components, which we describe next. Collectively, all the hardware and software components shown in the figure form the *platform*. Where we draw

26

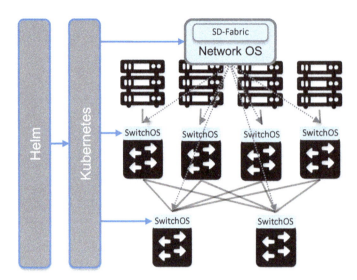

Figure 1: Example building block components used to construct a cloud, including commodity servers and switches, interconnected by a leaf-spine switching fabric.

the line between what's *in the platform* and what runs *on top of the platform*, and why it is important, will become clear in later chapters. The summary is that one mechanism is responsible for bringing up the platform and preparing it to host workloads, and a different mechanism is responsible for managing the various workloads that are deployed on that platform.

1.3.2 Software Building Blocks

We assume four foundational software technologies, all running on the commodity processors in the cluster:

1. Linux provides isolation for running container workloads.

2. Docker containers package software functionality.

3. Kubernetes instantiates and interconnects containers.

4. Helm charts specify how collections of related containers are interconnected to build applications.

These are all well known and ubiquitous, and so we only summarize them here. Links to related information for anyone who is not familiar with them (including excellent hands-on tutorials for the three container-related building blocks) are given below.

Linux is the OS that runs on the bare metal systems. It provides low-level APIs that container runtime systems use to implement isolation, including *namespaces* to isolate filesystem and network access, and *cgroups* to limit memory and processor usage.

Docker is a container runtime that leverages OS isolation APIs to instantiate and run multiple containers, each of which is an instance defined by a Docker image. Docker images are most frequently built using a Dockerfile, which uses a layering approach that allows sharing and building customized images on top of base images. A final image for a particular task incorporates all dependencies required by the software that is to run in the container, resulting in a container image that is portable across servers, depending only on the kernel and Docker runtime. We also assume one or more image artifact repositories of Docker containers that we will want to deploy in our cloud, of which `https://hub.docker.com/` is the best known example.

Further Reading:
Docker Tutorial (`https://www.docker.com/101-tutorial`).

Kubernetes is a container management system. It provides a programmatic interface for scaling container instances up and down, allocating server resources to them, setting up virtual networks to interconnect those instances, and opening service ports that external clients can use to access those instances. Behind the scenes, Kubernetes monitors the liveness of those containers, and automatically restarts any that have failed. In other words, if you instruct Kubernetes to spin up three instances of microservice X, Kubernetes will do its best to keep three instances of the container that implements X running at all times.

Kubernetes also provides mechanisms that can be used to configure microservices when they start up, including *ConfigMaps*, *Secrets*, and *Operators*. Because of the role they play in cloud management, we discuss these mechanisms in more detail as they are introduced.

Further Reading:
Kubernetes Tutorial (`https://kubernetes.io/docs/tutorials/kubernetes-basics/`).

Helm is a configuration set manager that runs on top of Kubernetes. It issues calls against the Kubernetes API according to an operator-provided specification, known as a *Helm Chart*. It is now common practice for cloud applications built from a set of microservices to publish a Helm chart that defines how the application is to be deployed on a Kubernetes cluster. See `https://artifacthub.io/` for a collection of publicly available Helm Charts.

Further Reading:
Helm Tutorial (`https://helm.sh/docs/intro/quickstart/`).

The cloud management software described in this book is available in the form of a set of Docker containers, plus the associated Helm Charts that specify how they are to be deployed in a Kubernetes cluster. Overall, we make use of over 20 such open source software packages in the chapters that follow. Our goal is to show how all these open building blocks can be assembled into a comprehensive cloud management platform. We describe each tool in enough detail to appreciate how all the parts fit together—providing end-to-end coverage by connecting all the dots—plus links to full documentation for those who want to dig deeper into the details.

1.3.3 Switching Fabric

We assume the cloud is constructed using an SDN-based switching fabric, with a disaggregated control plane running in the same cloud as the fabric interconnects. For the purpose of this book, we assume the following SDN software stack:

- A Network OS hosts a set of control applications, including a control application that manages the leaf-spine switching fabric. We use ONOS as an open source exemplar Network OS. ONOS, in turn, hosts the SD-Fabric control app.

- A Switch OS runs on each switch, providing a northbound gNMI and gNOI interface through which the Network OS controls and configures each switch. We use Stratum as an open source exemplar Switch OS.

Building a cloud using an SDN-based switching fabric is a best practice adopted by hyperscaler cloud providers. Their solutions remain proprietary, so we use ONOS and Stratum as open source examples. It is noteworthy that ONOS and Stratum are both packaged as Docker containers, and so can be orchestrated (on *both* servers and switches) by Kubernetes and Helm.[5]

[5] Switches often include a commodity processor, typically running Linux and hosting control software, in addition to any switching chip that implements the data plane. Stratum runs on this processor, and exports a northbound API that ONOS uses to configure and control the switch.

1.3.4 Repositories

For completeness, we need to mention that nearly every mechanism described in this book takes advantage of cloud-hosted repositories, such as GitHub (for code), DockerHub (for Docker images), and ArtifactHub (for Helm charts). We also assume complementary systems like Gerrit, which layer a code-review mechanism on top of a Git repository, but having direct experience with Gerrit is not critical to understanding the material.

1.3.5 Other Options

Just as important as what building blocks we take for granted are the technologies we do not include. We discuss three here.

First, you might have expected Service Mesh frameworks like Istio or Linkerd to be included. While it is true that anyone running applications on top of Kubernetes might decide to use Istio or Linkerd to help do that job—and this includes us, since much of the management system described in this book is implemented as a set of microservices—we happen to not take that approach. This is primarily an engineering choice: Service Meshes provide more features than we need, and correspondingly, we are able to realize the necessary functionality using more narrowly focused mechanisms. There is also a pedagogical reason: The fine-grained components we use are more consistent with our goal of identifying the elemental pieces of operations and management, rather than having those components bundled in a comprehensive package. We do, however, return to the role of service meshes in our discussion of observability in Chapter 6.

Further Reading:
GitHub Tutorial (https://guides.github.com/activities/hello-world/).

Gerrit Code Review (https://www.gerritcodereview.com/).

What's the Master Plan?

There is a general issue of how one makes engineering choices about the combination of software packages to use in a cloud-based system like the one this book describes. Ignoring the plethora of commercial offerings, just the number of open source projects at the Linux Foundation and the Apache Foundation available to help you build and operate a cloud is (by our count) approaching 100. These projects are largely independent, and in many cases, competing for mind-share. This results in significant overlap in functionality, with any Venn diagram you try to draw constantly shifting over time.

This is all to say, there is no master plan for what a cloud management stack should look like. If you start with component X as the centerpiece of your approach—perhaps because it solves your most immediate problem—you will end up adding dozens of other components over time to fully complete the system. Moreover, the end result will likely look different from the system someone else constructs starting with component Y. There simply is no consensus framework for which you get to select a component from column A, a second complementary component from column B, and so on. This is also true for the Aether managed service we use as an exemplar.

This makes it all the more important that we take a first principles approach, which starts by identifying the set of requirements and exploring the design space. Only as a final step do we select an existing software component. This approach naturally results in an end-to-end solution that assembles many smaller components, and tends to avoid bundled/multi-faceted solutions. This does not inoculate us from having to evolve the system over time, but it does help to approach the topic with visibility into the full scope and complexity of the design space. And even if one ends up adopting a bundled solution, understanding all the trade-offs being made under the covers will help to make a more informed decision.

Second, we assume a container-based cloud platform. An alternative would have been VM-based. The main reason for this choice is that containers are rapidly becoming the de facto way to deploy scalable and highly available functionality, and operationalizing such functionality in enterprises is our primary use case. Containers are sometimes deployed inside of VMs (rather than directly on physical machines), but in that case, the VMs can be viewed as part of the underlying infrastructure (rather than a service that is offered to users). Another way of saying this is that this book focuses on how to operationalize a Platform-as-a-Service (PaaS) rather than an

Infrastructure-as-a-Service (IaaS), although later chapters will describe how to introduce VMs as an optional way to provision the underlying infrastructure for that PaaS.

Finally, the Aether edge cloud we use as an example is similar to many other cloud platforms being built to support on-prem deployments. The dominant use case shifts over time—with Artificial Intelligence (AI) recently overtaking Internet-of-Things (IoT) as the most compelling justification for edge clouds—but the operational challenge remains the same. For example, *Open Edge Platform* recently open sourced by Intel includes example AI applications and a collection of AI libraries, but also an *Edge Management Framework* that mirrors the one describe this book. It starts with a Kubernetes foundation, and includes tools for provisioning edge servers, orchestrating edge clusters using those servers, lifecycle managing edge applications, and enabling observability. Many of the engineering choices are the same as in Aether (some are different), but the important takeaway is that Kubernetes-based edge clouds are quickly becoming commonplace. That's the reason they are such a good case study.

1.4 Future of the Sysadmin

System administrators have been responsible for operating enterprise networks since the first file servers, client workstations, and LANs were deployed over 30 years ago. Throughout that history, a robust vendor ecosystem has introduced an increasingly diverse set of network appliances, compounding the challenge of the sysadmin's job. The introduction of virtualization technology led to server consolidation, but did not greatly reduce the management overhead. This is because each virtual appliance remains in a management silo.

Cloud providers, because of the scale of the systems they build, cannot survive with operational silos, and so they introduced increasingly sophisticated cloud orchestration technologies. Kubernetes and Helm are two high-impact examples. These cloud best practices are now available to enterprises as well, but they are often bundled as a managed service, with the cloud provider playing an ever-greater role in operating the enterprise's services. Outsourcing portions of the IT

Further Reading:
Open Edge Platform (https://github.com/open-edge-platform/).

Edge Management Framework (https://github.com/open-edge-platform/edge-manageability-framework).

responsibility to a cloud provider is an attractive value proposition for many enterprises, but comes with the risk of increased dependence on a single provider. This equation is complicated by the increased likelihood that Mobile Network Operators (MNOs) also participate in the rollout of private 5G connectivity within the enterprise, deployed as yet another cloud service.

The approach this book takes is to explore a best-of-both-worlds opportunity. It does this by walking you through the collection of subsystems, and associated management processes, required to operationalize an on-premises cloud, and then provide on-going support for that cloud and the services it hosts (including 5G connectivity). Our hope is that understanding what's under the covers of cloud-managed services will help enterprises better share responsibility for managing their IT infrastructure with cloud providers, and potentially with MNOs.

Chapter 2: Architecture

This chapter identifies all the subsystems that go into building and operationalizing a cloud capable of running an assortment of cloud native services. We use Aether to illustrate specific design choices, and so we start by describing why an enterprise might install a system like Aether in the first place.

Aether is a Kubernetes-based edge cloud, augmented with a 5G-based connectivity service. Aether is targeted at enterprises that want to take advantage of 5G connectivity in support of mission-critical edge applications requiring predictable, low-latency connectivity. In short, "Kubernetes-based" means Aether is able to host container-based services, and "5G-based connectivity" means Aether is able to connect those services to mobile devices throughout the enterprise's physical plant. This combination of features to support deployment of edge applications, coupled with Aether being offered as a managed service, means Aether can fairly be characterized as a Platform-as-a-Service (PaaS).

Aether supports this combination by implementing both the RAN and the user plane of the Mobile Core on-prem, as cloud native workloads co-located on the Aether cluster. This is often referred to as *local breakout* because it enables direct communication between mobile devices and edge applications without data traffic leaving the enterprise. This scenario is depicted in Figure 2, which does not name the edge applications, but substituting Internet-of-Things (IoT) would be an illustrative example.

PaaS for Industry 4.0

Edge clouds like Aether are an important component of a trend called Industry 4.0: A combination of intelligent devices, robust wireless connectivity, and cloud-based AI/ML capabilities, all working together to enable software-based optimization and innovation.

Connecting industry assets to the cloud has the potential to bring transformative benefits. This starts with collecting deep operational data on assets and infrastructure, from sensors, video feeds and telemetry from machinery. It also includes applying ML to this data to gain insights, identify patterns and predict outcomes (e.g., when a device is likely to fail), followed by automating industrial processes so as to minimize human intervention and enable remote operations (e.g., power optimization, idling quiescent machinery). In general, the goal is to create an IT foundation for continually improving industrial operations through software.

As for why we refer to Aether as a PaaS for such use cases, the answer is somewhat subjective. Generally, a PaaS offers more than virtualized compute and storage (that is what IaaS does), and includes additional layers of "middleware" to enable application developers to deploy their applications without dealing with all the intricacies of managing the underlying infrastructure. In the case of Aether, the platform includes support for 5G connectivity, including an API that edge apps can use to customize that connectivity to better meet their objectives. This does not preclude also loading an ML-platform or an IoT-platform onto Aether, further enhancing the application support it provides.

The approach includes both edge (on-prem) and centralized (off-prem) components. This is true for edge apps, which often have a centralized counterpart running in a commodity cloud. It is also true for the 5G Mobile Core, where the on-prem User Plane (UP) is paired with a centralized Control Plane (CP). The central cloud shown in this figure might be private (i.e., operated by the enterprise), public (i.e., operated by a commercial cloud provider), or some combination of the two (i.e., not all centralized elements need to run in the same cloud).

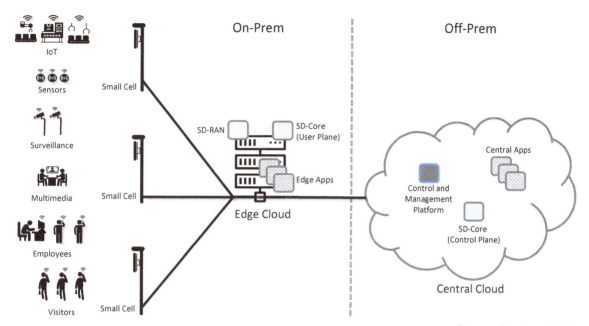

Figure 2: Overview of Aether as a hybrid cloud, with edge apps and the 5G data plane (called local breakout) running on-prem and various management and control-related workloads running in a central cloud.

Also shown in Figure 2 is a centralized *Control and Management Platform*. This represents all the functionality needed to offer Aether as a managed service, with system administrators using a portal exported by this platform to operate the underlying infrastructure and services within their enterprise. The rest of this book is about everything that goes into implementing that *Control and Management Platform*.

2.1 Edge Cloud

The edge cloud, which in Aether is called ACE (Aether Connected Edge), is a Kubernetes-based cluster similar to the one shown in Figure 1 of Chapter 1. It is a platform that consists of one or more server racks interconnected by a leaf-spine switching fabric, with an SDN control plane (denoted SD-Fabric) managing the fabric.

As shown in Figure 3, ACE hosts two additional microservice-based subsystems on top of this platform; they collectively implement *5G-Connectivity-as-a-Service*. The first subsystem, SD-RAN, is an SDN-based implementation of the 5G Radio Access Network (RAN). It con-

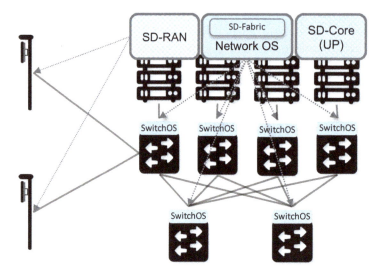

Figure 3: Aether Connected Edge (ACE) = The cloud platform (Kubernetes and SD-Fabric) plus the 5G connectivity service (RAN and User Plane of Mobile Core). Dotted lines (e.g., between SD-RAN and the individual base stations, and between the Network OS and the individual switches) represent control relationships (e.g., SD-RAN controls the small cells and SD-Fabric controls the switches).

trols the small cell base stations deployed throughout the enterprise. The second subsystem, SD-Core, is an SDN-based implementation of the User Plane half of the Mobile Core. It is responsible for forwarding traffic between the RAN and the Internet. The SD-Core Control Plane (CP) runs off-site, and is not shown in Figure 3. Both subsystems (as well as the SD-Fabric), are deployed as a set of microservices, but details about the functionality implemented by these containers is otherwise not critical to this discussion. For our purposes, they are representative of any cloud native workload. (The interested reader is referred to our companion 5G and SDN books for more information about the internal working of SD-RAN, SD-Core, and SD-Fabric.)

Once ACE is running in this configuration, it is ready to host a collection of edge applications (not shown in Figure 3), and as with any Kubernetes-based cluster, a Helm chart would be the preferred way to deploy such applications. What's unique to ACE is the ability to connect such applications to mobile devices throughout the enterprise using the 5G Connectivity Service implemented by SD-RAN and SD-Core. This service is offered as a managed service, with enterprise system administrators able to use a programmatic API (and associated GUI portal) to control that service; that is, authorize devices, restrict

Further Reading:
L. Peterson and O. Sunay. 5G Mobile Networks: A Systems Approach. March 2020.

L. Peterson, *et al.* Software-Defined Networks: A Systems Approach. November. 2021.

access, set Quality-of-Service parameters for different devices and applications, and so on. How to provide such a runtime control interface is the topic of Chapter 5.

2.2 Hybrid Cloud

While it is possible to instantiate a single ACE cluster in just one site, Aether is designed to support multiple ACE deployments, all of which are managed from the central cloud. Such a hybrid cloud scenario is depicted in Figure 4, which shows two subsystems running in the central cloud: (1) one or more instances of the Mobile Core Control Plane (CP), and (2) the Aether Management Platform (AMP).

Each SD-Core CP controls one or more SD-Core UPs, as specified by 3GPP, the standards organization responsible for 5G. Exactly how CP instances (running centrally) are paired with UP instances (running at the edges) is a runtime decision, and depends on the degree of isolation the enterprise sites require. AMP is responsible for managing all the centralized and edge subsystems (as introduced in the next section).

Figure 4: Aether runs in a hybrid cloud configuration, with Control Plane of Mobile Core and the Aether Management Platform (AMP) running in the Central Cloud.

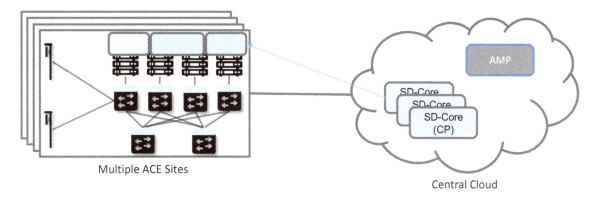

Multiple ACE Sites

Central Cloud

There is an important aspect of this hybrid cloud that is not obvious from Figure 4, which is that the "hybrid cloud" we keep referring to is best described as a set of Kubernetes clusters, rather than a set of physical clusters (similar to the one we started with in Figure 1 of Chapter 1). This is because, while each ACE site usually corresponds to a physical cluster built out of bare-metal components, each of the SD-Core CP subsystems shown in Figure 4 is actually deployed in a logical Kubernetes cluster on a commodity cloud. The same is true for AMP. Aether's centralized components are able to run in Google Cloud Platform, Microsoft Azure, and Amazon's AWS. They can also run as an emulated cluster implemented by a system like KIND—Kubernetes in Docker—making it possible for developers to run these components on their laptops.

To be clear, Kubernetes adopts generic terminology, such as "cluster" and "service", and gives it a very specific meaning. In Kubernetes-speak, a *Cluster* is a logical domain in which Kubernetes manages a set of containers. This "Kubernetes cluster" may have a one-to-one relationship with an underlying physical cluster, but it is also possible that a Kubernetes cluster is instantiated inside a datacenter, as one of potentially thousands of such logical clusters. And as we'll see in a later chapter, even an ACE edge site sometimes hosts more than one Kubernetes cluster, for example, one running production services and one used for trial deployments of new services.

2.3 Stakeholders

With the understanding that our target environment is a collection of Kubernetes clusters—some running on bare-metal hardware at edge sites and some running in central datacenters—there is an orthogonal issue of how decision-making responsibility for those clusters is shared among multiple stakeholders. Identifying the relevant stakeholders is an important prerequisite for establishing a cloud service, and while the example we use may not be suitable for all situations, it does illustrate the design implications.

For Aether, we care about two primary stakeholders: (1) the *cloud operators* who manage the hybrid cloud as a whole, and (2) the *enterprise users* who decide on a per-site basis how to take advantage of the local cloud resources (e.g., what edge applications to run and how to slice connectivity resources among those apps). We sometimes call the latter "enterprise admins" to distinguish them from "end-users" who might want to manage their own personal devices.

The architecture is multi-tenant in the sense that it authenticates and isolates these stakeholders, allowing each to access only those objects they are responsible for. This makes the approach agnostic as to whether all the edge sites belong to a single organization (with that organization also responsible for operating the cloud), or alternatively, there being a separate organization that offers a managed service to a set of distinct enterprises (each of which spans one or more sites). The architecture can also accommodate end-users, and provide them with a "self-service" portal, but we do not elaborate on that possibility.

There is a potential third stakeholder of note—third-party service providers—which points to the larger issue of how we deploy and manage additional edge applications. To keep the discussion tangible—but remaining in the open source arena—we use OpenVINO as an illustrative example. OpenVINO is a framework for deploying AI inference models. It is interesting in the context of Aether because one of its use cases is processing video streams, for example to detect and count people who enter the field of view of a collection of 5G-connected cameras.

On the one hand, OpenVINO is just like the 5G-related components we're already incorporating into our hybrid cloud: it is deployed as a Kubernetes-based set of microservices. On the other hand, we have to ask who is responsible for managing it, which is to say "who operationalizes OpenVINO?"

One answer is that the operators who already manage the rest of the hybrid cloud also manage the collection of edge applications added to cloud. Enterprise admins might activate and control those apps on a site-by-site basis, but it is the operations team already responsible for provisioning, deploying, and managing those edge clouds that also does the same for OpenVINO and any other applications that run on that cloud. Generalizing from one edge service (5G connectivity) to arbitrarily many edge services has implications for control and management (which we'll discuss throughout the book), but fundamentally nothing changes in the course we've already set out for ourselves.

Having the cloud operator *curate and manage* a set of edge services is the assumption Aether makes (and we assume throughout this

Further Reading:
OpenVINO Toolkit
(https://docs.openvino.ai).

book), but for completeness, we take note of two other possibilities. One is that we extend our hybrid architecture to support independent third-party service providers. Each new edge service acquires its own isolated Kubernetes cluster from the edge cloud, and then the 3rd-party provider takes over all responsibility for managing the service running in that cluster. From the perspective of the cloud operator, though, the task just became significantly more difficult because the architecture would need to support Kubernetes as a managed service, which is sometimes called *Containers-as-a-Service (CaaS)*.[6] Creating isolated Kubernetes clusters on-demand is a step further than we take things in this book, in part because there is a second possible answer that seems more likely to happen.

This second approach is that a multi-cloud emerges *within* enterprises. Today, most people equate multi-cloud with services running across multiple hyperscalers, but with edge clouds becoming more common, it seems likely that enterprises will invite multiple edge clouds onto their local premises, some hyperscaler-provided and some not, each hosting a different subset of edge services. For example, one edge cloud might host a 5G connectivity service and another might host an AI platform like OpenVINO. The question this raises is whether the cloud management technologies described in this book still apply in that setting. The answer is yes: the fundamental management challenges remain the same. The main difference is knowing when to directly control a Kubernetes cluster (as we do in this book) and when to do so indirectly through the manager for that cluster. There are also new problems that are unique to multi-clouds, such as inter-cloud service discovery, but they are beyond the scope of this book.

2.4 Control and Management

We are now ready to describe the architecture of the Aether Management Platform (AMP), which as shown in Figure 5, manages both the distributed set of ACE clusters and the other control clusters running in the central cloud. And illustrating the recursive nature of the management challenge, AMP is also responsible for managing AMP!

[6] This is not strictly an either-or-situation. It is possible to curate an edge service, provision cluster resources for it, but then delegate operational responsibility to a 3rd-party service provider.

AMP includes one or more portals targeted at different stakeholders, with Figure 5 showing the two examples we focus on in this book: a User Portal intended for enterprise admins who need to manage services delivered to a local site, and an Operations Portal intended for the ops team responsible for keeping Aether up to date and running smoothly. Again, other stakeholders (classes of users) are possible, but this distinction does represent a natural division between those who *use* cloud services and those who *operate* cloud services.

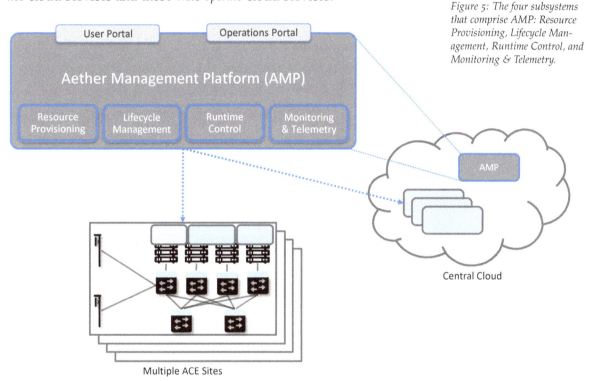

Figure 5: The four subsystems that comprise AMP: Resource Provisioning, Lifecycle Management, Runtime Control, and Monitoring & Telemetry.

We do not focus on these portals, which provide a graphical interface to a subset of AMP functionality, but we instead describe the aggregate functionality supported by AMP, which is organized around four subsystems:

- Resource Provisioning: Responsible for initializing and configuring resources (e.g., servers, switches) that add, replace, or upgrade capacity for Aether.

- Lifecycle Management: Responsible for continuous integration and deployment of software functionality available on Aether.

- Runtime Control: Responsible for the ongoing configuration and control of the services (e.g., connectivity) provided by Aether.

- Monitoring & Telemetry: Responsible for collecting, archiving, evaluating, and analyzing telemetry data generated by Aether components.

Internally, each of these subsystems is implemented as a highly available cloud service, running as a collection of microservices. The design is cloud-agnostic, so AMP can be deployed in a public cloud (e.g., Google Cloud, AWS, Azure), an operator-owned Telco cloud, (e.g, AT&T's AIC), or an enterprise-owned private cloud. For the pilot deployment of Aether, AMP runs in the Google Cloud.

The rest of this section introduces these four subsystems, with the chapters that follow filling in more detail about each.

2.4.1 Resource Provisioning

Resource Provisioning configures and bootstraps resources (both physical and virtual), bringing them up to a state so Lifecycle Management can take over and manage the software running on those resources. It roughly corresponds to Day 0 operations, and includes both the hands-on aspect of installing and physically connecting hardware, and the inventory-tracking required to manage physical assets.

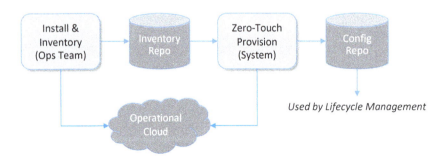

Figure 6: High-level overview of Resource Provisioning.

Figure 6 gives a high-level overview. As a consequence of the operations team physically connecting resources to the cloud and recording attributes for those resources in an Inventory Repo, a Zero-Touch Provisioning system (a) generates a set of configuration artifacts that are stored in a Config Repo and used during Lifecycle Management, and (b) initializes the newly deployed resources so they are in a state that Lifecycle Management is able to control. The idea of storing configuration directives in a Repo, like any other code module, is a practice known as *Configuration-as-Code*, and we will see it applied in different ways throughout this book.

Recall from Chapter 1 that we called out the "Aether platform" as distinct from the cloud native workloads that are hosted on the platform. This is relevant here because Resource Provisioning has to get this platform up and running before Lifecycle Management can do its job. But in another example of circular dependencies, Lifecycle Management also plays a role in keeping the underlying platform up to date.

Clearly, the "Install & Inventory" step requires human involvement, and some amount of hands-on resource-prep is necessary, but the goal is to minimize the operator configuration steps (and associated expertise) and maximize the automation carried out by the Zero-Touch Provisioning system. Also realize that Figure 6 is biased towards provisioning a physical cluster, such as the edge sites in Aether. For a hybrid cloud that also includes one or more virtual clusters running in central datacenters, it is necessary to provision those virtual resources as well. Chapter 3 describes provisioning from this broader perspective, considering both physical and virtual resources.

2.4.2 *Lifecycle Management*

Lifecycle Management is the process of integrating debugged, extended, and refactored components (often microservices) into a set of artifacts (e.g., Docker containers and Helm charts), and subsequently deploying those artifacts to the operational cloud. It includes a comprehensive testing regime, and typically, a procedure by which developers inspect and comment on each others' code.

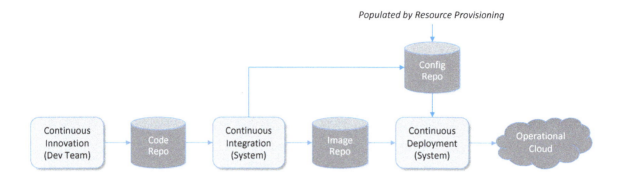

Figure 7: High-level overview of Lifecycle Management.

Figure 7 gives a high-level overview, where it is common to split the integration and deployment phases, the latter of which combines the integration artifacts from the first phase with the configuration artifacts generated by Resource Provisioning described in the previous subsection. The figure does not show any human intervention (after development), which implies any patches checked into the code repo trigger integration, and any new integration artifacts trigger deployment. This is commonly referred to as Continuous Integration / Continuous Deployment (CI/CD), although in practice, operator discretion and other factors are also taken into account before deployment actually happens.

One of the key responsibilities of Lifecycle Management is version control, which includes evaluating dependencies, but also the possibility that it will sometimes be necessary to both roll out new versions of software and rollback to old versions, as well as operate with multiple versions deployed simultaneously. Managing all the configuration state needed to successfully deploy the right version of each component in the system is the central challenge, which we address in Chapter 4.

2.4.3 Runtime Control

Once deployed and running, Runtime Control provides a programmatic API that can be used by various stakeholders to manage whatever abstract service(s) the system offers (e.g., 5G connectivity in the case of Aether). As shown in Figure 8, Runtime Control partially addresses the "management silo" issue raised in Chapter 1, so users do not need to know that connectivity potentially spans four different components, or how to control/configure each of them individually. (Or, as in the case of the Mobile Core, that SD-Core is distributed across two clouds, with the CP sub-part responsible for controlling the UP sub-part.) In the case of the connectivity service, for example, users only care about being able to authorize devices and set QoS parameters on an end-to-end basis.

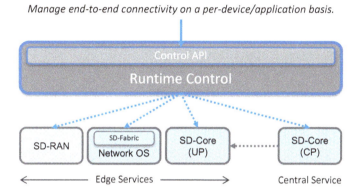

Figure 8: Example use case that requires ongoing runtime control.

Note that Figure 8 focuses on Connectivity-as-a-Service, but the same idea applies to all services the cloud offers to end users. Thus, we can generalize the figure so Runtime Control mediates access to any of the underlying microservices (or collections of microservices) the cloud designer wishes to make publicly accessible, including the rest of AMP! In effect, Runtime Control implements an abstraction layer, codified with a programmatic API.

Given this mediation role, Runtime Control provides mechanisms to model (represent) the abstract services to be offered to users; store any configuration and control state associated with those models; apply that state to the underlying components, ensuring they remain in sync with the operator's intentions; and authorize the set of API calls that users try to invoke on each service. These details are spelled out in Chapter 5.

2.4.4 Monitoring and Telemetry

In addition to controlling service functionality, a running system has
to be continuously monitored so that operators can diagnose and
respond to failures, tune performance, do root cause analysis, perform
security audits, and understand when it is necessary to provision
additional capacity. This requires mechanisms to observe system
behavior, collect and archive the resulting data, analyze the data and
trigger various actions in response, and visualize the data in human
consumable dashboards (similar to the example shown in Figure 9).

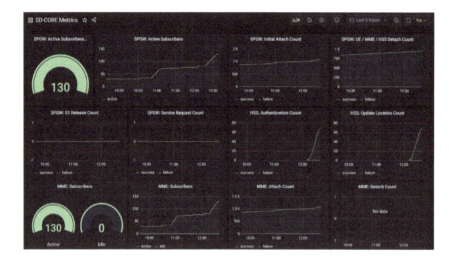

Figure 9: Example Aether dashboard, showing the health of one of the subsystems (SD-Core).

In broad terms, it is common to think of this aspect of cloud management as having three parts: a monitoring component that collects
quantitative metrics (e.g., load averages, transmission rates, ops per
second); a logging component that collects diagnostic messages (i.e.,
text strings explaining various event); and a tracing component that
can reconstruct workflows through a set of microservices. All include
a timestamp, so it is possible to link quantitative analysis with qualitative explanations in support of diagnostics and analytics.

2.4.5 Summary

This overview of the management architecture could lead one to conclude that these four subsystems were architected, in a rigorous, top-down fashion, to be completely independent. But that is not the case. It is more accurate to say that the system evolved bottom up, solving the next immediate problem one at a time, all the while creating a large ecosystem of open source components that can be used in different combinations. What this book presents is a retrospective description of the end result, organized into four subsystems to help make sense of it all.

There are, in practice, many opportunities for interactions among the four components, and in some cases, there are overlapping concerns that lead to considerable debate. This is what makes operationalizing a cloud such a thorny problem. For example, it's difficult to draw a crisp line between where resource provisioning ends and lifecycle management begins. One could view provisioning as "Step 0" of lifecycle management. As another example, the runtime control and monitoring subsystems are often combined in a single user interface, giving operators a way to both read (monitor) and write (control) various parameters of a running system. Connecting those two subsystems is how we build closed loop control.

These two "simplifications" allow us to reduce the architectural overview of the management platform to the two-dimensional representation shown in Figure 10. In one dimension, layered on top of the hybrid cloud being managed, is the Runtime Control system (including Monitoring and Telemetry to close the control loop). Users and Operators read and write parameters of the running system via a well-defined REST API. In the other dimension, running beside the hybrid cloud, is the Lifecycle Management system (including Resource Provisioning as Step 0). Operators and Developers specify changes to the system by checking code (including configuration specs) into a repo, and then periodically triggering an upgrade of the running system.

This simplified perspective draws attention to an ambiguity, which is the distinction between "changes to the parameters of a running

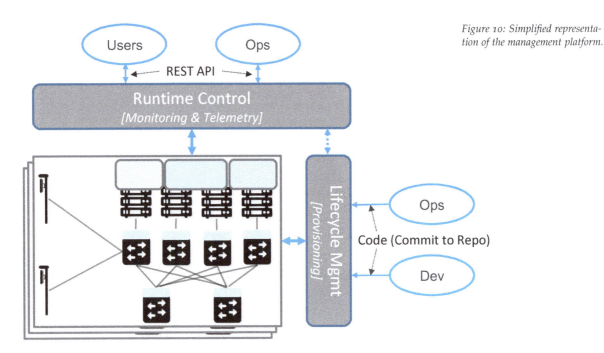

Figure 10: Simplified representation of the management platform.

system" versus "upgrading the system that is running." Generally, Lifecycle Management takes responsibility for *configuring* each component (including what version of each component is deployed), while runtime control takes responsibility for *controlling* each component. But where you draw the line between configuration and control is somewhat arbitrary. Do configuration changes only happen when you first boot a component, or can you change the configuration of a running system, and if you do, how does that differ from changing a control parameter? And as suggested by the dotted arrow in Figure 10, is there value in having Runtime Control instigate changes via Lifecycle Management? The difference is usually related to frequency of change (which is in turn related to how disruptive to existing traffic/workload the change is), but ultimately it doesn't matter what you call it, as long as the mechanisms you use meet all of your requirements.

Of course, an operational system doesn't tolerate such ambiguities very well. Each aspect of management has to be supported in a well-defined, efficient and repeatable way. That's why we include a description of a concrete realization of each of the four subsystems, reflecting one particular set of design choices. We call out the opportunities to make different engineering decisions, along with the design rationale behind our choices, as we add more details in the chapters that follow.

2.5 DevOps

The preceding discussion focuses on the subsystems that make up the Control and Management Platform, but such a platform is used by people. This implies the need for a set of operational processes and procedures, which in a cloud setting, are now commonly organized around the DevOps model. The following gives a high-level summary, with a more extensive discussion of ops-related procedures presented throughout the book.

DevOps has become an overused term, generally taken to mean that the line between the engineers who develop cloud functionality and the operators who deploy and manage cloud functionality is blurred, with the same team responsible for both. But that definition is too imprecise to be helpful. There are really three aspects of DevOps that are important to understand.

First, when it comes to a set of services (or user-visible features), it is true that the developers play a role in deploying and operating those services. Enabling them to do that is exactly the value of the Management Platform. Consider the team responsible for SD-RAN in Aether, as an example. That team not only implements new SD-RAN features, but once their patch sets are checked into the code repository, those changes are integrated and deployed by the automated toolchain introduced in the previous section. This means the SD-RAN team is also responsible for:

1. Adding test cases to the CI half of Lifecycle Management, and writing any configuration specifications needed by the CD half of Lifecycle Management.

2. Instrumenting their code so it reports into the Monitoring and

Telemetry framework, giving them the dashboards and alarms they need to troubleshoot any problems that arise.

3. Augmenting the data model of Runtime Control, so their component's internal interfaces are plumbed through to the cloud's externally visible Northbound Interface.

Once deployed and operational, the SD-RAN team is also responsible for diagnosing any problems that cannot be resolved by a dedicated "on call" support staff.[7] The SD-RAN team is motivated to take advantage of the platform's automated mechanisms (rather than exploit short-term workarounds), and to document their component's behavior (especially how to resolve known problems), so they do not get support calls in the middle of the night.

> ### Experience at Google
>
> *Our brief sketch of DevOps is based on how the approach is practiced at Google, and in this context, it is a great example of how good things come from efforts to minimize toil. As Google gained experience building and running its cloud, the incremental improvements to their cloud management system were assimilated in a system known as Borg.*
>
> *Kubernetes, the open source project widely used across the industry today, was spun out of Borg. The functionality embodied by Kubernetes evolved over time to deal with the operational challenges of deploying, upgrading, and monitoring a set of containers, serving as a great example of how a "rising tide lifts all boats." Given enough time, it may be the case that next layer of cloud management machinery, roughly corresponding to the topics covered in this book, will also be taken as a given. The challenge, as we will see, is the multi-dimensional scope of the problem.*

Second, all of the activity outlined in the previous paragraph is possible only because of the rich set of capabilities built into the Control and Management Platform that is the subject of this book.[8] Someone had to build that platform, which includes a testing framework that individual tests can be plugged into; an automated deployment

[7] Whether traditional or DevOps-based, there is typically a front-line support team, which is often said to provide Tier-1 support. They interact directly with customers and are the first to respond to alarms, resolving the issue according to a well-scripted playbook. If Tier-1 support is not able to resolve an issue, it is elevated to Tier-2 and eventually Tier-3, the latter of which is the developers who best understand implementation details.

[8] This we why we refer to the management system as a "platform", with AMP as an illustrative example. It serves as a common framework that developers of all the other cloud components can plug into and leverage. This is how you ultimately address the "management silo" problem.

framework that is able to roll upgrades out to a scalable number of servers and sites without manual intervention; a monitoring and telemetry framework that components can report into; a runtime control environment that can translate high-level directives into low-level operations on backend components; and so on. While each of these frameworks was once created by a team tasked with keeping some other service running smoothly, they have taken on a life of their own. The Control and Management Platform now has its own DevOps team(s), who in addition to continually improving the platform, also field operational events, and when necessary, interact with other teams (e.g., the SD-RAN team in Aether) to resolve issues that come up. They are sometimes called Site Reliability Engineers (SREs), and in addition to being responsible for the Control and Management Platform, they enforce operational discipline—the third aspect of DevOps discussed next—on everyone else.

Finally, when operating with discipline and rigor, all of these teams strictly adhere to two quantitative rules. The first balances *feature velocity* with *system reliability*. Each component is given an *error budget* (percentage of time it can be down), and new features cannot be rolled out unless the corresponding component has been operating within this bound. This test is a "gate" on the CI/CD pipeline. The second rule balances how much time is spent on *operational toil* (time spent by a human diagnosing or fixing problems) with time spent engineering new capabilities into the Control and Management Platform to reduce future toil. If too much time is spent toiling and too little time is spent making the Control and Management Platform better, then it is taken as a sign that additional engineering resources are needed.

Further Reading:
B. Beyer, C. Jones, J. Petoff, and N. Murphy, Editors. Site Reliability Engineering: How Google Runs Production Systems, 2016.

Chapter 3: Resource Provisioning

Resource Provisioning is the process of bringing virtual and physical resources online. It has both a hands-on component (racking and connecting devices) and a bootstrap component (configuring how the resources boot into a "ready" state). Resource Provisioning happens when a cloud deployment is first installed—i.e., an initial set of resources are provisioned—but also incrementally over time as new resources are added, obsolete resources are removed, and out-of-date resources are upgraded.

The goal of Resource Provisioning is to be zero-touch, which is impossible for hardware resources because it includes an intrinsically manual step. (We take up the issue of provisioning virtual resources in a moment.) Realistically, the goal is to minimize the number and complexity of configuration steps required beyond physically connecting the device, keeping in mind that we are starting with commodity hardware received directly from a vendor, and not a plug-and-play appliance that has already been prepped.

When a cloud is built from virtual resources (e.g., VMs instantiated on a commercial cloud) the "rack and connect" step is carried out by a sequence of API calls rather than a hands-on technician. Of course, we want to automate the sequence of calls needed to activate virtual infrastructure, which has inspired an approach known as *Infrastructure-as-Code*, a special case of the *Configuration-as-Code* concept introduced in Chapter 2. The general idea is to document, in a declarative format that can be "executed", exactly what our infrastructure is to look like; how it is to be configured. Aether uses Terraform as its approach to Infrastructure-as-Code.

When a cloud is built from a combination of virtual and physical resources, as is the case for a hybrid cloud like Aether, we need a seamless way to accommodate both. To this end, our approach is to first overlay a *logical structure* on top of hardware resources, making them roughly equivalent to the virtual resources we get from a commercial cloud provider. This results in a hybrid scenario similar to the one shown in Figure 11. NetBox is our open source solution for layering this logical structure on top of physical hardware. NetBox also helps us address the requirement of tracking physical inventory.

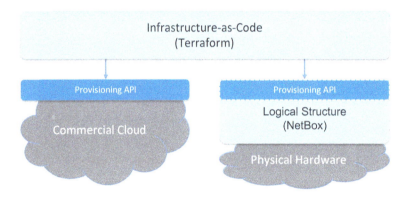

Figure 11: Resource Provisioning in a hybrid cloud that includes both physical and virtual resources.

Note that the Provisioning API shown on the right in Figure 11 is *not* the NetBox API. Terraform does not interact directly with NetBox, but instead with artifacts left behind by the hardware provisioning process described in Section 3.1. One way to think about this is that the task of booting hardware into the "ready" state involves installing and configuring several subsystems that collectively form the cloud platform. It is this platform that Terraform interacts with, using an API we describe at the end of Section 3.1.

This chapter describes both sides of Figure 11 starting with provisioning physical infrastructure. Our approach is to focus on the challenge of provisioning an entire site the first time. We comment on the simpler problem of incrementally provisioning individual resources as relevant details emerge.

3.1 Physical Infrastructure

The process of stacking and racking hardware is inherently human-intensive, and includes considerations such as airflow and cable management. These issues are beyond the scope of this book. We focus instead on the "physical/virtual" boundary, which starts with the cabling plan that a hands-on technician uses as a blueprint. The details of such a plan are highly deployment-specific, but we use the example shown in Figure 12 to help illustrate all the steps involved. The example is based on Aether clusters deployed in enterprises, which serves to highlight the required level of specificity. Considerable planning is required to specify an appropriate *Bill of Materials (BOM)*, including details about individual device models, but this aspect of the problem is also outside our scope.

Figure 12: Example network cable plan for an edge cluster.

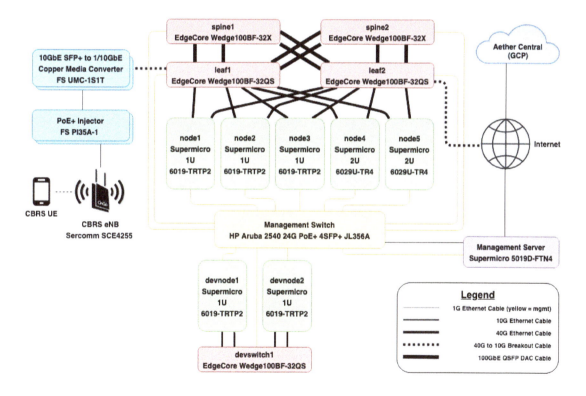

The blueprint shown in Figure 12 actually includes two logical clusters sharing a Management Switch and a Management Server. The upper cluster corresponds to a production deployment, and includes five servers and a 2x2 leaf-spine switching fabric. The lower cluster is for development, and includes two servers and a single switch. Defining such logical groupings of hardware resources is not unique to Aether; we can ask a commercial cloud provider to provision multiple logical clusters, so being able to do the same on physical resources is a natural requirement.

In addition to following this blueprint, the technician also enters various facts about the physical infrastructure into a database. This information, which is used in later provisioning steps, is where we pick up the story.

3.1.1 Document Infrastructure

Documenting the physical infrastructure's logical structure in a database is how we cross the physical-to-virtual divide. It involves both defining a set of models for the information being collected (this schema effectively represents the logical structure shown in Figure 11), and entering the corresponding facts about the physical devices. This process is familiar to anyone who is responsible for managing a network of devices, whether it is the first stage in a larger automated framework (such as the one described in this book) or simply a place to record what IP address has been assigned to each network appliance.

There are several open source tools available for this task. Our choice is NetBox. It supports IP address management (IPAM); inventory-related information about types of devices and where they are installed; how infrastructure is organized (racked) by group and site; and how devices are connected to consoles, networks, and power sources. More information is readily available on the NetBox web site.

One of the key features of NetBox is the ability to customize the set of models used to organize all the information that is collected. For example, an operator can define physical groupings like *Rack* and *Site*, but also logical groupings like *Organization* and *Deployment*.[9] In

Further Reading:
NetBox: Information Resource Modeling Application (`https://docs.netbox.dev`).

[9] In this section, we denote models and model fields in italics (e.g., *Site*, *Address*) and specific values assigned to an instance of a model as a constant (e.g., 10.0.0.0/22).

the following we use the Aether cable plan shown in Figure 12 as an illustrative example, focusing on what happens when provisioning a single Aether site (but keeping in mind that Aether spans multiple sites, as outlined in Chapter 2).

The first step is to create a record for the site being provisioned, and document all the relevant metadata for that site. This includes the *Name* and *Location* of the *Site*, along with the *Organization* the site belongs to. An *Organization* can have more than one *Site*, while a *Site* can (a) span one or more *Racks*, and (b) host one or more *Deployments*. A *Deployment* is a logical cluster, corresponding, for example, to Production, Staging, and Development. The cabling plan shown in Figure 12 includes two such deployments.

This is also the time to specify the VLANs and IP Prefixes assigned to this particular edge deployment. Because it is important to maintain a clear relationship between VLANs, IP Prefixes, and DNS names (the last of which are auto-generated), it is helpful to walk through the following concrete example. We start with the minimal set of VLANs needed per Site:

- ADMIN 1

- UPLINK 10

- MGMT 800

- FABRIC 801

These are Aether-specific, but they illustrate the set of VLANs a cluster might need. Minimally, one would expect to see a "management" network (MGMT in this example) and a "data" network (FABRIC in this example) in any cluster. Also specific to Aether (but generally applicable), if there are multiple Deployments at a Site sharing a single management server, additional VLANs (incremented by 10 for MGMT/FABRIC) are added. For example, a second Development deployment might define:

- DEVMGMT 810

- DEVFABRIC 811

IP Prefixes are then associated with VLANs, with all edge IP prefixes fitting into a /22 sized block. This block is then partitioned in a way that works in concert with how DNS names are managed; i.e., names are generated by combining the first <devname> component of the *Device* names (see below) with this suffix. Using 10.0.0.0/22 as an example, there are four edge prefixes, with the following purposes:

- ADMIN Prefix 10.0.0.0/25 (for IPMI)

    - Has the Management Server and Management Switch

    - Assign the ADMIN 1 VLAN

    - Set domain to admin.<deployment>.<site>.aetherproject.net

- MGMT Prefix 10.0.0.128/25 (for infrastructure control plane)

    - Has the Server Management plane, Fabric Switch Management

    - Assign MGMT 800 VLAN

    - Set domain to mgmt.<deployment>.<site>.aetherproject.net

- FABRIC Prefix 10.0.1.0/25 (for infrastructure data plane)

    - IP addresses of the qsfp0 port of the Compute Nodes to Fabric switches, plus other Fabric-connected devices (e.g., eNB)

    - Assign FABRIC 801 VLAN

    - Set domain to fab1.<deployment>.<site>.aetherproject.net

- FABRIC Prefix 10.0.1.128/25 (for infrastructure data plane)

    - IP addresses of the qsfp1 port of the Compute Nodes to fabric switches

    - Assign FABRIC 801 VLAN

    - Set domain to fab2.<deployment>.<site>.aetherproject.net

There are other edge prefixes used by Kubernetes, but they do not need to be created in NetBox. Note that qsfp0 and qsfp1 in this example denote transceiver ports connecting the switching fabric, where *QSFP* stands for Quad (4-channel) Small Form-factor Pluggable.

With this site-wide information recorded, the next step is to install and document each *Device*. This includes entering a <devname>, which is subsequently used to generate a fully qualified domain name for the device: <devname>.<deployment>.<site>.aetherproject.net. The following fields are also filled in when creating a Device:

• Site

• Rack & Rack Position

• Manufacturer

• Model

• Serial number

• Device Type

• MAC Addresses

Note there is typically both a primary and a management (e.g., BMC/IPMI) interface. One convenience feature of NetBox is to use the *Device Type* as a template that sets the default naming of interfaces, power connections, and other equipment model specific attributes.

Finally, the virtual interfaces for the Device must be specified, with its *Label* field set to the physical network interface that it is assigned. IP addresses are then assigned to the physical and virtual interfaces we have defined. The Management Server should always have the first IP address in each range, and they should be incremental, as follows:

• Management Server

  – eno1 - site provided public IP address, or blank if DHCP pro-vided

  – eno2 - 10.0.0.1/25 (first of ADMIN) - set as primary IP

  – bmc - 10.0.0.2/25 (next of ADMIN)

  – mgmt800 - 10.0.0.129/25 (first of MGMT, on VLAN 800)

  – fab801 - 10.0.1.1/25 (first of FABRIC, on VLAN 801)

- Management Switch

  - gbe1 - 10.0.0.3/25 (next of ADMIN) - set as primary IP

- Fabric Switch

  - eth0 - 10.0.0.130/25 (next of MGMT), set as primary IP

  - bmc - 10.0.0.131/25

- Compute Server

  - eth0 - 10.0.0.132/25 (next of MGMT), set as primary IP

  - bmc - 10.0.0.4/25 (next of ADMIN)

  - qsfp0 - 10.0.1.2/25 (next of FABRIC)

  - qsfp1 - 10.0.1.3/25

- Other Fabric devices (eNB, etc.)

  - eth0 or other primary interface - 10.0.1.4/25 (next of FABRIC)

Once this data is entered into NetBox, it can be used to generate a rack diagram, similar to the one shown in Figure 13, corresponding to the cabling diagram shown in Figure 12. Note that the diagram shows two logical *Deployments* (Production and Development), co-located in one physical rack.

It is also possible to generate other useful specifications for the deployment, helping the technician confirm the recorded logical specification matches the actual physical representation. For example, Figure 14 shows the set of cables and how they connect the set of hardware in our example deployment.

If all of this seems like a tedious amount of detail, then you get the main point of this section. Everything about automating the control and management of a cloud hinges on having complete and accurate data about its resources. Keeping this information in sync with the reality of the physical infrastructure is often the weakest link in this process. The only saving grace is that the information is highly structured, and tools like NetBox help us codify this structure.

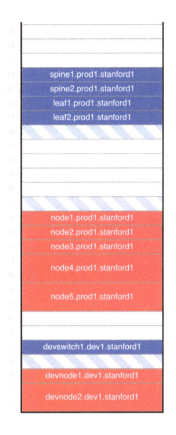 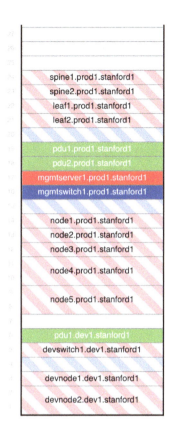

Figure 13: NetBox rendering of rack configuration.

3.1.2 Configure and Boot

After installing the hardware and recording the relevant facts about the installation, the next step is to configure and boot the hardware so that it is "ready" for the automated procedures that follow. The goal is to minimize manual configuration required to onboard physical infrastructure like that shown in Figure 12, but *zero-touch* is a high bar. To illustrate, the bootstrapping steps needed to complete provisioning for our example deployment include:

- Configure the Management Switch to know the set of VLANs being used.

- Configure the Management Server so it boots from a provided USB key.

Cables

	ID	Label	Side A	Termination A	Side B	Termination B	Status	Type	Length	Color
☐	165	—	mgmtswitch1.prod1.stanford1	gbe3	node1.prod1.stanford1	bmc	Connected	CAT6	2 Feet	
☐	166	—	mgmtswitch1.prod1.stanford1	gbe4	node2.prod1.stanford1	bmc	Connected	CAT6	2 Feet	
☐	167	—	mgmtswitch1.prod1.stanford1	gbe5	node3.prod1.stanford1	bmc	Connected	CAT6	2 Feet	
☐	168	—	mgmtswitch1.prod1.stanford1	gbe6	node4.prod1.stanford1	bmc	Connected	CAT6	3 Feet	
☐	169	—	mgmtswitch1.prod1.stanford1	gbe7	node5.prod1.stanford1	bmc	Connected	CAT6	3 Feet	
☐	170	—	mgmtswitch1.prod1.stanford1	gbe11	spine1.prod1.stanford1	eth0	Connected	CAT6	5 Feet	
☐	171	—	mgmtswitch1.prod1.stanford1	gbe12	spine2.prod1.stanford1	eth0	Connected	CAT6	5 Feet	
☐	172	—	mgmtswitch1.prod1.stanford1	gbe13	leaf1.prod1.stanford1	eth0	Connected	CAT6	5 Feet	
☐	173	—	mgmtswitch1.prod1.stanford1	gbe14	leaf2.prod1.stanford1	eth0	Connected	CAT6	5 Feet	
☐	174	—	mgmtswitch1.prod1.stanford1	gbe15	node1.prod1.stanford1	gbe0	Connected	CAT6	2 Feet	
☐	175	—	mgmtswitch1.prod1.stanford1	gbe16	node2.prod1.stanford1	gbe0	Connected	CAT6	2 Feet	
☐	176	—	mgmtswitch1.prod1.stanford1	gbe17	node3.prod1.stanford1	gbe0	Connected	CAT6	2 Feet	
☐	177	—	mgmtswitch1.prod1.stanford1	gbe18	node4.prod1.stanford1	gbe0	Connected	CAT6	3 Feet	
☐	178	—	mgmtswitch1.prod1.stanford1	gbe19	node5.prod1.stanford1	gbe0	Connected	CAT6	3 Feet	

Figure 14: NetBox report of cabling.

- Run Ansible playbooks needed to complete configuration onto the Management Server.

- Configure the Compute Servers so they boot from the Management Server (via iPXE).

- Configure the Fabric Switches so they boot from the Management Server (via Nginx).

- Configure the eNBs (mobile base stations) so they know their IP addresses.

These are all manual configuration steps, requiring either console access or entering information into a device web interface, such that any subsequent configuration steps can be both fully automated and resilient. Note that while these steps cannot be automated away, they do not necessarily have to be performed in the field; hardware shipped to a remote site can first be prepped accordingly. Also note that care should be taken to *not* overload this step with configuration that can be done later. For example, various radio parameters can be set on the eNBs when it is physically installed, but those parameters will become settable through the Management Platform once the cluster is brought online.

Manual configuration work done at this stage should be minimized, and most systems should use automated means of configuration. For example, using DHCP pervasively with MAC reservations for IP address assignment instead of manual configuration of each interface allows for management to be zero-touch and simplifies future reconfiguration.

The automated aspects of configuration are implemented as a set of Ansible *roles* and *playbooks*, which in terms of the high-level overview shown in Figure 6 of Chapter 2, corresponds to the box representing the *"Zero-Touch Provision (System)"*. Said another way, there is no off-the-shelf ZTP solution we can use (i.e., someone has to write the playbooks), but the problem is greatly simplified by having access to all the configuration parameters that NetBox maintains.

The general idea is as follows. For every network service (e.g., DNS, DHCP, Nginx) and every per-device subsystem (e.g., network interfaces, Docker) that needs to be configured, there is a corresponding Ansible role (set of related playbooks). These configurations are applied to the Management Server during the manual configuration stage summarized above, once the management network is online.

The Ansible playbooks install and configure the network services on the Management Server. The role of DNS and DHCP are obvious. As for iPXE and Nginx, they are used to bootstrap the rest of the infrastructure. The compute servers are configured by iPXE delivered over DHCP/TFTP, and then load the scripted OS installation from an Nginx web server. The fabric switches load their Stratum OS package from Nginx.

In many cases, the playbooks use parameters—such as VLANs, IP addresses, DNS names, and so on—extracted from NetBox. Figure 15 illustrates the approach, and fills in a few details. For example, a home-grown Python program (edgeconfig.py) extracts data from NetBox using the REST API and outputs a corresponding set of YAML files, crafted to serve as input to Ansible, which creates yet more configuration on the management and compute systems. One example of

64

this is the *Netplan* file, which is used in Ubuntu to manage network interfaces. More information about Ansible and Netplan can be found on their respective web sites.

Further Reading:
Ansible: Automation Platform
(https://www.ansible.com/).

Netplan: Network Configuration Abstraction Renderer
(https://netplan.io).

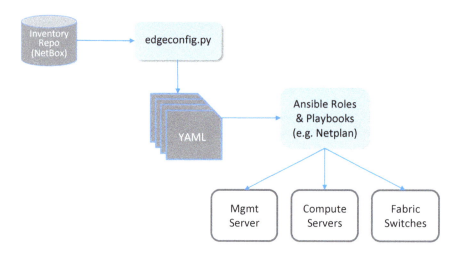

Figure 15: Configuring network services and OS-level subsystems using NetBox data.

While Figure 15 highlights how Ansible is paired with Netplan to configure kernel-level details, there is also an Ansible playbook that installs Docker on each compute server and fabric switch, and then launches a Docker container running a "finalize" image. This image makes calls into the next layer of the provisioning stack, effectively signaling that the cluster is running and ready for further instructions. We are now ready to describe that next layer of the stack.

3.1.3 Provisioning API

As a result of the steps described so far, we can assume each server and switch is up and running, but we still have a little work to do to prepare our bare-metal clusters for the next layer in the provisioning stack, essentially establishing parity between the left- and right-hand sides of the hybrid cloud shown in Figure 11. If you ask yourself *"What would Google do?"* this reduces to the task of setting up a GCP-like API for the bare-metal edge clouds. This API primarily subsumes the Kubernetes API, but it goes beyond providing a way to *use* Kubernetes to also include calls to *manage* Kubernetes.

In short, this "manage Kubernetes" task is to turn a set of inter-connected servers and switches into a fully-instantiated Kubernetes cluster. For starters, the API needs to provide a means to install and configure Kubernetes on each physical cluster. This includes specifying which version of Kubernetes to run, selecting the right combination of Container Network Interface (CNI) plugins (virtual network adaptors), and connecting Kubernetes to the local network (and any VPNs it might need). This layer also needs to provide a means to set up accounts (and associated credentials) for accessing and using each Kubernetes cluster, and a way to manage independent projects that are to be deployed on a given cluster (i.e., manage namespaces for multiple applications).

As an example, Aether uses Rancher to manage Kubernetes on the bare-metal clusters, with one centralized instance of Rancher being responsible for managing all the edge sites. This results in the configuration shown in Figure 16, which to emphasize Rancher's scope, shows multiple edge clusters. Although not shown in the Figure, the GCP-provided API, just like Rancher, also spans multiple physical sites (e.g., us-west1-a, europe-north1-b, asia-south2-c, and so on).

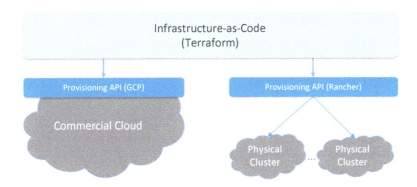

Figure 16: Provisioning in a hybrid cloud that includes an API layer for managing Kubernetes running on multiple bare-metal clusters.

We conclude this discussion by noting that while we often treat Kubernetes as though it is an industry-wide standard, that is not quite the reality of the situation. Each cloud provider offers its own customized version:

• Microsoft Azure offers the Azure Kubernetes Service (AKS)

- AWS offers the Amazon Elastic Kubernetes Service (EKS)

- Google Cloud offers the Google Kubernetes Engine (GKE)

- Aether edges run the Rancher-certified version of Kubernetes (RKE)

Although the *CNCF (Cloud Native Computing Foundation)*—the open source organization responsible for shepherding the Kubernetes project—certifies these and other versions of Kubernetes, this only establishes baseline compliance. Each version if free to enhance their offering beyond this baseline, and these enhancements often take the form of additional features for provisioning and controlling a Kubernetes cluster. Our job at the cloud management layer is to provide operators with a means to manage this heterogeneity. And as we'll see in Section 3.2, this is the primary challenge addressed by the Infrastructure-as-Code layer.

3.1.4 Provisioning VMs

We conclude our discussion of the steps required to provision physical machines by considering the implications of provisioning virtual machines, or VMs. That's something that happens "behind the scenes" when you request a Kubernetes cluster from AKS, EKS, or GKE, but that's because the hyperscalers have the option of layering their Kubernetes service on top of their Infrastructure-as-a-Service (IaaS). Do we need something similar for the edge cloud we're building?

Not necessarily. Because our goal is to support a curated set of edge services that provide value to our enterprise users, and not to support Container-as-a-Service so untrusted third-parties can spin up whatever applications they want, we do not need to manage VMs "as a service." But we still may want to use VMs as a way to isolate Kubernetes workloads on a limited number of physical servers. This can be done as a provisioning step, akin to connecting and booting a physical machine, but using virtualization mechanisms like KVM and Proxmox. There is no need for a full-fledged IaaS mechanism, such as OpenStack. These VMs would then be recorded as first-class cloud resource in NetBox and the other tools described in this section, no different from a physical machine.

The unanswered question is why one might decide to do that, considering that Kubernetes already allows us to deploy multiple applications on a single cluster. One reason is to support fine-grained resource isolation, making it possible to (a) ensure that each Kubernetes application receives the processor, memory, and storage resources it needs to do its job, and (b) reduce the risk of information leaking between the applications. Suppose, for example, that in addition to SD-Fabric, SD-RAN and SD-Core workloads that run (by default) on each edge site, we also want to run one or more other edge apps, such as the OpenVINO platform introduced in Section 2.3. To ensure that there is no interference between these applications, we could dedicate a subset of physical servers to each of them. Physical partitioning is a coarse-grained way to share the physical cluster. Being able to "split" one or more servers between multiple uses—by instantiating VMs—gives the operator more flexibility in allocating resources, which usually translates into requiring fewer overall resources. Note that there are other ways to specify how cluster resources are shared between applications (which we will see in Section 4.4), but the provisioning layer is one place where the issue can be addressed.

3.2 Infrastructure-as-Code

The provisioning interface for each of the Kubernetes variants just described includes a programmatic API, a Command Line Interface (CLI), and a Graphical User Interface (GUI). If you try any of the tutorials we recommended throughout this book, you'll likely use one of the latter two. For operational deployments, however, having a human operator interact with a CLI or GUI is problematic. This is not only because humans are error-prone, but also because it's nearly impossible to consistently repeat a sequence of configuration steps. Being able to continuously repeat the process is at the heart of Lifecycle Management described in the next chapter.

The solution is to find a declarative way of saying what your infrastructure is to look like—what set of Kubernetes clusters (e.g., some running at the edges on bare-metal and some instantiated in GCP) are to be instantiated, and how each is to be configured—and then automate the task of making calls against the programmatic API to make it so. This is the essence of Infrastructure-as-Code, and as we've already said, Terraform is our open source example.

Since Terraform specifications are declarative, the best way to understand them is to walk through a specific example. In doing so, our goal isn't to document Terraform (online documentation and step-by-step tutorials are available for those those interested in more detail), but rather, to build some intuition about the role this layer plays in managing a cloud.

To make sense of the example, the main thing you need to know about the Terraform configuration language is that it provides a means to both (1) specify *templates* for different kinds of resources (these are .tf files), and (2) fill in the *variables* for specific instances of those resource templates (these are .tfvars files). Then given a set of .tf and tfvars files, Terraform implements a two-stage process. In the first stage it constructs an execution plan, based on what has changed since the previous plan it executed. In the second stage, Terraform carries out the sequence of tasks required to bring the underlying infrastructure "up to spec" with the latest definition. Note that our job, for now, is the write these specification files, and check them into the Config Repo. Terraform gets invoked as part of the CI/CD pipeline described in Chapter 4.

Now to the specific files. At the top-most level, the operator defines the set of *providers* they plan to incorporate into their infrastructure. We can think of each provider as corresponding to a cloud backend, including the corresponding provisioning API depicted in Figure 16. In our example, we show only two providers: the Rancher-managed edge clusters and the GCP-managed centralized clusters. Note that the example file declares a set of relevant variables for each provider (e.g., url, access-key), which are "filled in" in by instance-specific variable files described next.

Further Reading:
Terraform Documentation
(https://www.terraform.io/docs).

```
terraform {
  required_version = ">= 0.13"
  required_providers {
    rancher2 = {
```

```
      source  = "rancher/rancher2"
      version = "= 1.15.1"
    }
    google = {
      source  = "hashicorp/google"
      version = "~> 3.65.0"
    }
    null = {
      source  = "hashicorp/null"
      version = "~> 2.1.2"
    }
  }
}

variable "rancher" {
  description = "Rancher credential"
  type = object({
    url        = string
    access_key = string
    secret_key = string
  })
}

variable "gcp_config" {
  description = "GCP project and network configuration"
  type = object({
    region          = string
    compute_project = string
    network_project = string
    network_name    = string
    subnet_name     = string
  })
}

provider "rancher2" {
  api_url    = var.rancher.url
  access_key = var.rancher.access_key
  secret_key = var.rancher.secret_key
}

provider "google" {
```

```
    # Provide GCP credential using GOOGLE_CREDENTIALS variable
    project = var.gcp_config.compute_project
    region  = var.gcp_config.region
}
```

The next step is to fill in the details (define values) for the actual set of clusters we want to provision. Let's look at two examples, corresponding to the two providers we just specified. The first shows a GCP-provided cluster (named amp-gcp) that is to host the AMP workload. (There's a similar sdcore-gcp that hosts an instance of the SD-Core.) The labels associated with this particular cluster (e.g., env = "production") establish linkage between Terraform (which assigns the label to each cluster it instantiates) and other layers of the management stack (which selectively take different actions based on the associated labels). We'll see an example of these labels being used in Section 4.4.

```
cluster_name = "amp-gcp"
cluster_nodes = {
  amp-us-west2-a = {
    host       = "10.168.0.18"
    roles      = ["etcd", "controlplane", "worker"]
    labels     = []
    taints     = []
  },
  amp-us-west2-b = {
    host       = "10.168.0.17"
    roles      = ["etcd", "controlplane", "worker"]
    labels     = []
    taints     = []
  },
  amp-us-west2-c = {
    host       = "10.168.0.250"
    roles      = ["etcd", "controlplane", "worker"]
    labels     = []
    taints     = []
  }
}
cluster_labels = {
  env          = "production"
  clusterInfra = "gcp"
```

```
    clusterRole  = "amp"
    k8s          = "self-managed"
    backup       = "enabled"
  }
```

The second example shows an edge cluster (named ace-X) to be in-stantiated at *Site X*. As shown in the example code, this is a bare-metal cluster consisting of five servers and four switches (two leaf switches and two spine switches). The address for each device must match the one assigned during the hardware-provisioning stage outlined in Section 3.1. Ideally, the NetBox (and related) tool chain described in that section would auto-generate these Terraform variables files, but in practice, manually entering the data is often still necessary.

```
cluster_name  = "ace-X"
cluster_nodes = {
  leaf1 = {
    user        = "terraform"
    private_key = "~/.ssh/id_rsa_terraform"
    host        = "10.64.10.133"
    roles       = ["worker"]
    labels      = ["node-role.aetherproject.org=switch"]
    taints      = ["node-role.aetherproject.org=switch:NoSchedule"]
  },
  leaf2 = {
    user        = "terraform"
    private_key = "~/.ssh/id_rsa_terraform"
    host        = "10.64.10.137"
    roles       = ["worker"]
    labels      = ["node-role.aetherproject.org=switch"]
    taints      = ["node-role.aetherproject.org=switch:NoSchedule"]
  },
  spine1 = {
    user        = "terraform"
    private_key = "~/.ssh/id_rsa_terraform"
    host        = "10.64.10.131"
    roles       = ["worker"]
    labels      = ["node-role.aetherproject.org=switch"]
    taints      = ["node-role.aetherproject.org=switch:NoSchedule"]
  },
```

```
spine2 = {
  user        = "terraform"
  private_key = "~/.ssh/id_rsa_terraform"
  host        = "10.64.10.135"
  roles       = ["worker"]
  labels      = ["node-role.aetherproject.org=switch"]
  taints      = ["node-role.aetherproject.org=switch:NoSchedule"]
},
server-1 = {
  user        = "terraform"
  private_key = "~/.ssh/id_rsa_terraform"
  host        = "10.64.10.138"
  roles       = ["etcd", "controlplane", "worker"]
  labels      = []
  taints      = []
},
server-2 = {
  user        = "terraform"
  private_key = "~/.ssh/id_rsa_terraform"
  host        = "10.64.10.139"
  roles       = ["etcd", "controlplane", "worker"]
  labels      = []
  taints      = []
},
server-3 = {
  user        = "terraform"
  private_key = "~/.ssh/id_rsa_terraform"
  host        = "10.64.10.140"
  roles       = ["etcd", "controlplane", "worker"]
  labels      = []
  taints      = []
},
server-4 = {
  user        = "terraform"
  private_key = "~/.ssh/id_rsa_terraform"
  host        = "10.64.10.141"
  roles       = ["worker"]
  labels      = []
  taints      = []
},
server-5 = {
```

```
    user        = "terraform"
    private_key = "~/.ssh/id_rsa_terraform"
    host        = "10.64.10.142"
    roles       = ["worker"]
    labels      = []
    taints      = []
  }
}
cluster_labels = {
  env           = "production"
  clusterInfra  = "bare-metal"
  clusterRole   = "ace"
  k8s           = "self-managed"
  coreType      = "4g"
  upfType       = "up4"
}
```

The final piece of the puzzle is to to fill in the remaining details about exactly how each Kubernetes cluster is to be instantiated. In this case, we show just the RKE-specific module used to configure the edge clusters, where most of the details are straightforward if you understand Kubernetes. For example, the module specifies that each edge cluster should load the calico and multus CNI plugins. It also defines how to invoke kubectl to configure Kubernetes according to these specifications. Less familiar, all references to SCTPSupport indicate whether or not that particular Kubernetes cluster needs to support SCTP, a Telco-oriented network protocol that is not included in a vanilla Kubernetes deployment, but is needed by the SD-Core.

```
terraform {
  required_providers {
    rancher2 = {
      source  = "rancher/rancher2"
    }
    null = {
      source  = "hashicorp/null"
      version = "~> 2.1.2"
    }
  }
}
```

```
resource "rancher2_cluster" "cluster" {
  name = var.cluster_config.cluster_name

  enable_cluster_monitoring = false
  enable_cluster_alerting   = false

  labels = var.cluster_labels

  rke_config {
    kubernetes_version = var.cluster_config.k8s_version

    authentication {
      strategy = "x509"
    }

    monitoring {
      provider = "none"
    }

    network {
      plugin = "calico"
    }

    services {
      etcd {
        backup_config {
          enabled        = true
          interval_hours = 6
          retention      = 30
        }
        retention = "72h"
        snapshot  = false
      }

      kube_api {
        service_cluster_ip_range = var.cluster_config.k8s_cluster_ip_range
        extra_args = {
          feature-gates = "SCTPSupport=True"
        }
      }
```

```
      kubelet {
        cluster_domain     = var.cluster_config.cluster_domain
        cluster_dns_server = var.cluster_config.kube_dns_cluster_ip
        fail_swap_on       = false
        extra_args = {
          cpu-manager-policy = "static"
          kube-reserved      = "cpu=500m,memory=256Mi"
          system-reserved    = "cpu=500m,memory=256Mi"
          feature-gates      = "SCTPSupport=True"
        }
      }

      kube_controller {
        cluster_cidr            = var.cluster_config.k8s_pod_range
        service_cluster_ip_range = var.cluster_config.k8s_cluster_ip_range
        extra_args = {
          feature-gates = "SCTPSupport=True"
        }
      }

      scheduler {
        extra_args = {
          feature-gates = "SCTPSupport=True"
        }
      }

      kubeproxy {
        extra_args = {
          feature-gates = "SCTPSupport=True"
          proxy-mode    = "ipvs"
        }
      }
    }
    addons_include = ["https://raw.githubusercontent.com/multus-cni/3.7/images/daemonset.yml"]
    addons = var.addon_manifests
  }
}

resource "null_resource" "nodes" {
  triggers = {
```

```
    cluster_nodes = length(var.nodes)
  }

  for_each = var.nodes

  connection {
    type                = "ssh"

    bastion_host        = var.bastion_host
    bastion_private_key = file(var.bastion_private_key)
    bastion_user        = var.bastion_user

    user        = each.value.user
    host        = each.value.host
    private_key = file(each.value.private_key)
  }

  provisioner "remote-exec" {
    inline = [<<EOT
      ${rancher2_cluster.cluster.cluster_registration_token[0].node_command} \
      ${join(" ", formatlist("--%s", each.value.roles))} \
      ${join(" ", formatlist("--taints %s", each.value.taints))} \
      ${join(" ", formatlist("--label %s", each.value.labels))}
      EOT
    ]
  }
}

resource "rancher2_cluster_sync" "cluster-wait" {
  cluster_id = rancher2_cluster.cluster.id

  provisioner "local-exec" {
    command = <<EOT
      kubectl set env daemonset/calico-node \
        --server ${yamldecode(rancher2_cluster.cluster.kube_config).clusters[0].cluster.server} \
        --token ${yamldecode(rancher2_cluster.cluster.kube_config).users[0].user.token} \
        --namespace kube-system \
          IP_AUTODETECTION_METHOD=${var.cluster_config.calico_ip_detect_method}
    EOT
  }
}
```

There are other loose ends that need to be tied up, such as defining the VPN to be used to connect edge clusters to their counterparts in GCP, but the above examples are sufficient to illustrate the role Infrastructure-as-Code plays in the cloud management stack. The key takeaway is that everything Terraform handles could have been done by a human operator making a sequence of CLI calls (or GUI clicks) on the backend Provisioning APIs, but experience has shown that approach to be error-prone and difficult to make consistently repeatable. Starting with declarative language and auto-generating the right sequence of API calls is a proven way to overcome that problem.

We conclude by drawing attention to the fact that while we now have a declarative specification for our cloud infrastructure, which we refer to as the *Aether Platform*, these specification files are yet another software artifact that we check into the Config Repo. This is what we mean by Infrastructure-as-Code: infrastructure specifications are checked into a repo and version-controlled like any other code. This repo, in turn, feeds the lifecycle management pipeline described in the next chapter. The physical provisioning steps described in Section 3.1 happen "outside" the pipeline (which is why we don't just fold resource provisioning into Lifecycle Management), but it is fair to think of resource provisioning as "Stage 0" of lifecycle management.

3.3 Platform Definition

The art of defining a system architecture, in our case a management framework for a hybrid cloud, is deciding where to draw the line between what's included inside the platform and what is considered an application running on top of the platform. For Aether, we have decided to include SD-Fabric inside the platform (along with Kubernetes), with SD-Core and SD-RAN treated as applications, even though all three are implemented as Kubernetes-based microservices. One consequence of this decision is that SD-Fabric is initialized as part of the provisioning system described in this chapter (with NetBox, Ansible, Rancher, and Terraform playing a role), whereas SD-Core and SD-RAN are deployed using the application-level mechanisms described in Chapter 4.

There may also be other edge applications running as Kubernetes workloads, which complicates the story because from their perspective, all of Aether (including the 5G connectivity that SD-Core and SD-RAN implements) is assumed to be part of the platform. In other words, Aether draws two lines, one demarcating Aether's base platform (Kubernetes plus SD-Fabric) and a second demarcating the Aether PaaS (which includes SD-Core and SD-RAN running on top of the platform, plus AMP managing the whole system). The distinction between "base platform" and "PaaS" is subtle, but essentially corresponds to the difference between a software stack and a managed service, respectively.

In some respects this is just a matter of terminology, which is certainly important, but the relevance to our discussion is that because we have multiple overlapping mechanisms at our disposal, giving us more than one way to solve each engineering problem we encounter, it is easy to end up with an implementation that unnecessarily conflates separable concerns. Being explicit and consistent about what is platform and what is application is a prerequisite for a sound overall design. It is also important to recognize the difference between an internal engineering decision (e.g., what mechanism is used to deploy a given component), and an externally-visible architectural decision (e.g., what functionality to expose through a public API).

Chapter 4: Lifecycle Management

Lifecycle Management is concerned with updating and evolving a running system over time. We have carved out the bootstrapping step of provisioning the hardware and installing the base software platform (Chapter 3), and so now we turn our attention to continually upgrading the software running on top of that platform. And as a reminder, we assume the base platform includes Linux running on each server and switch, plus Docker, Kubernetes, and Helm, with SD-Fabric controlling the network.

Traditionally, software would go through an offline integration and testing process before any effort to roll it out in production could begin. However, the approach taken in most modern cloud environments, including ours, is more expansive: it starts with the development process—the creation of new features and capabilities. Including the "innovation" step closes the virtuous cycle depicted in Figure 17, which the cloud industry has taught us leads to greater *feature velocity*.

Figure 17: Virtuous cycle with the goal of improving feature velocity.

Of course, not every enterprise has the same army of developers at their disposal that cloud providers do, but that does not shut them out of this opportunity. The innovation can come from many sources, including open source, so the real objective is to democratize the integration and deployment end of the pipeline. This is precisely the goal of the Lifecycle Management subsystem described in this chapter.

4.1 Design Overview

Figure 18 gives an overview of the pipeline/toolchain that make up
the two halves of Lifecycle Management—Continuous Integration
(CI) and Continuous Deployment (CD)—expanding on the high-
level introduction presented in Chapter 2. The key thing to focus
on is the Image and Config Repos in the middle. They represent the
"interface" between the two halves: CI produces Docker Images and
Helm Charts, storing them in the respective Repositories, while CD
consumes Docker Images and Helm Charts, pulling them from the
respective Repositories.

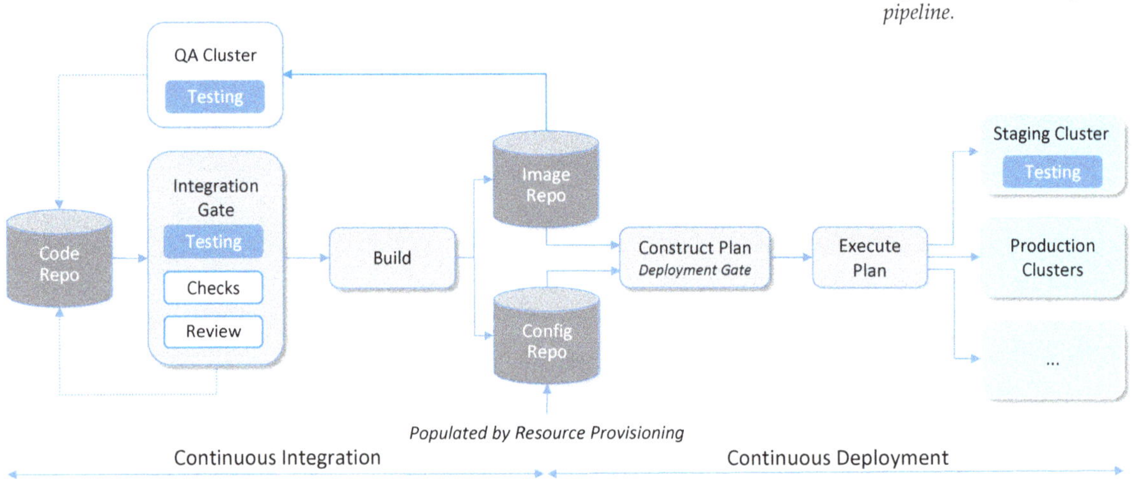

*Figure 18: Overview of the CI/CD
pipeline.*

The Config Repo also contains declarative specifications of the infrastructure artifacts produced by Resource Provisioning, specifically,
the Terraform templates and variable files.[10] While the "hands-on"
and "data entry" aspects of Resource Provisioning described in Section 3.1 happen outside the CI/CD pipeline, the ultimate output of
provisioning is the Infrastructure-as-Code that gets checked into the
Config Repo. These files are input to Lifecycle Management, which
implies that Terraform gets invoked as part of CI/CD whenever these
files change. In other words, CI/CD keeps both the software-related
components in the underlying cloud platform and the microservice
workloads that run on top of that platform up to date.

[10] We use the term "Config
Repo" generically to denote
one or more repositories
storing all the configuration-
related files. In practice,
there might be one repo for
Helm Charts and another for
Terraform Templates.

Continuous Delivery vs Deployment

You will also hear CD refer to "Continuous Delivery" instead of "Continuous Deployment", but we are interested in the complete end-to-end process, so CD will always imply the latter in this book. But keep in mind that "continuous" does not necessarily mean "instantaneous"; there can be a variety of gating functions injected into the CI/CD pipeline to control when and how upgrades get rolled out. The important point is that all the stages in the pipeline are automated.

So what exactly does "Continuous Delivery" mean? Arguably, it's redundant when coupled with "Continuous Integration" since the set of artifacts being produced by the CI half of the pipeline (e.g., Docker images) is precisely what's being delivered. There is no "next step" unless you also deploy those artifacts. It's hair-splitting, but some would argue CI is limited to testing new code and Continuous Delivery corresponds to the final "publish the artifact" step. For our purposes, we lump "publish the artifact" into the CI half of the pipeline.

There are three takeaways from this overview. The first is that by having well-defined artifacts passed between CI and CD (and between Resource Provisioning and CD), all three subsystems are loosely coupled, and able to perform their respective tasks independently. The second is that all authoritative state needed to successfully build and deploy the system is contained within the pipeline, specifically, as declarative specifications in the Config Repo. This is the cornerstone of *Configuration-as-Code* (also sometimes called *GitOps*), the cloud native approach to CI/CD that we are describing in this book. The third is that there is an opportunity for operators to apply discretion to the pipeline, as denoted by the *"Deployment Gate"* in the Figure, controlling what features get deployed when. This topic is discussed in the sidebar, as well as at other points throughout this chapter.

The third repository shown in Figure 18 is the Code Repo (on the far left). Although not explicitly indicated, developers are continually checking new features and bug fixes into this repo, which then triggers the CI/CD pipeline. A set of tests and code reviews are run

Further Reading:
Red Hat. An Illustrated Guide to GitOps (https://www.redhat.com/architect/illustrated-guide-gitops).

against these check-ins, with the output of those tests/reviews reported back to developers, who modify their patch sets accordingly. (These develop-and-test feedback loops are implied by the dotted lines in Figure 18.)

The far right of Figure 18 shows the set of deployment targets, with *Staging* and *Production* called out as two illustrative examples. The idea is that a new version of the software is deployed first to a set of Staging clusters, where it is subjected to realistic workloads for a period of time, and then rolled out to the Production clusters once the Staging deployments give us confidence that the upgrade is reliable.

This is a simplified depiction of what happens in practice. In general, there can be more than two distinct versions of the cloud software deployed at any given time. One reason this happens is that upgrades are typically rolled out incrementally (e.g., a few sites at a time over an extended period of time), meaning that even the production system plays a role in "staging" new releases. For example, a new version might first be deployed on 10% of the production machines, and once it is deemed reliable, is then rolled out to the next 25%, and so on. The exact rollout strategy is a controllable parameter, as described in more detail in Section 4.4.

Finally, two of the CI stages shown in Figure 18 identify a *Testing* component. One is a set of component-level tests that are run against each patch set checked into the Code Repo. These tests gate integration; fully merging a patch into the Code Repo requires first passing this preliminary round of tests. Once merged, the pipeline runs a build across all the components, and a second round of testing happens on a *Quality Assurance (QA)* cluster. Passing these tests gate deployment, but note that testing also happens in the Staging clusters, as part of the CD end of the pipeline. One might naturally wonder about the Production clusters. How do we continue to test the software after it is running in production? That happens, of course, but we tend to call it Monitoring & Telemetry (and subsequent diagnostics) rather than testing. This is the subject of Chapter 6.

We explore each of the stages in Figure 18 in more detail in the sections that follow, but as we dig into the individual mechanisms, it is helpful to keep a high-level, feature-centric perspective in the back of our minds. After all, the CI/CD pipeline is just an elaborate mechanism to help us manage the set of features we want our cloud to support. Each feature starts in development, which corresponds to everything left of the Integration Gate in Figure 18. Once a candidate feature is mature enough to be officially accepted into the main branch of the code repo (i.e., merged), it enters an integration phase, during which it is evaluated in combination with all the other candidate features, both new and old. Finally, whenever a given subset of features are deemed stable and have demonstrated value, they are deployed and finally run in production. Because of the centrality of testing throughout this entire lifetime of a set of features, we start there.

4.2 Testing Strategy

Our goal for Lifecycle Management is to improve feature velocity, but that always has to be balanced against delivering high-quality code—software that is reliable, scales, and meets performance requirements. Ensuring code quality requires that it be subjected to a battery of tests, but the linchpin for doing so "at speed" is the effective use of automation. This section introduces an approach to test automation, but we start by talking about the overall testing strategy.

The best practice for testing in the Cloud/DevOps environment is to adopt a *Shift Left* strategy, which introduces tests early in the development cycle, that is, on the left side of the pipeline shown in Figure 18. To apply this principle, you first have to understand what types of tests you need. Then you can set up the infrastructure required to automate those tests.

4.2.1 Categories of Tests

With respect to the types of tests, there is a rich vocabulary for talking about QA, but unfortunately, the definitions are often vague, overlapping, and not always uniformly applied. The following gives a simple taxonomy that serves our purposes, with different categories of tests organized according to the three stages of the CI/CD pipeline where they happen (relative to Figure 18):

- **Integration Gate:** These tests are run against every attempt to check in a patch set, and so must complete quickly. This means they are limited in scope. There are two categories of pre-merge tests:

  - **Unit Tests:** Developer-written tests that narrowly test a single module. The goal is to exercise as many code paths as possible by invoking "test calls" against the module's public interface.

  - **Smoke Tests:** A form of functional testing, typically run against a set of related modules, but in a shallow/superficial way (so they can run quickly). The etymology of the term "smoke tests" is said to come from hardware tests, as in, "does smoke come out of the box when you turn it on?"

- **QA Cluster:** These tests are run periodically (e.g., once day, once a week) and so can be more extensive. They typically test whole subsystems, or in some cases, the entire system. There are two categories of post-merge/pre-deploy tests:

  - **Integration Tests:** Ensures one or more subsystems function correctly, and adheres to known invariants. These tests exercise the integration machinery in addition to end-to-end (cross-module) functionality.

  - **Performance Tests:** Like functional tests in scope (i.e., at the subsystem level), but they measure quantifiable performance parameters, including the ability to scale the workload, rather than correctness.

- **Staging Cluster:** Candidate releases are run on the Staging cluster for an extensive period of time (e.g., multiple days) before being rolled out to Production. These tests are run against a complete and fully integrated system, and are often used to uncover memory leaks and other time-variant and workload-variant issues. There is just one category of tests run in this stage:

- **Soak Tests:** Sometimes referred to as *Canary Tests*, these require
  realistic workloads be placed on a complete system, through a
  combination of artificially generated traffic and requests from
  real users. Because the full system is integrated and deployed,
  these tests also serve to validate the CI/CD mechanisms, including for example, the specs checked into the Config Repo.

Figure 19 summaries the sequence of tests, highlighting the relationship among them across the lifecycle timeline. Note that the
leftmost tests typically happen repeatedly as part of the development
process, while the rightmost tests are part of the ongoing monitoring
of a production deployment. For simplicity, the figure shows the Soak
tests as running before deployment, but in practice, there is likely a
continuum whereby new versions of the system are incrementally
rolled out.

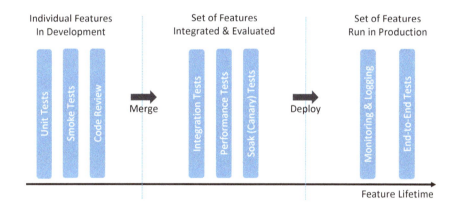

Figure 19: Sequence of tests along the feature timeline, as implemented by the CI/CD pipeline.

One of the challenges in crafting a testing strategy is deciding
whether a given test belongs in the set of Smoke tests that gate merging a patch, or the set of Integration tests that happen after a patch is
merged into the code repo, but before it is deployed. There is no hard-
and-fast rule; it's a balancing act. You want to test new software as
early as you realistically can, but full integration takes both time and
resources (i.e., a realistic platform for running the candidate software).
    Related to this trade-off, testing infrastructure requires a combina-
tion of virtual resources (e.g., VMs that are pre-configured with much

of the underlying platform already installed) and physical resources (e.g., small clusters that faithfully represent the eventual target hardware). Again, it's not a hard-and-fast rule, but early (Smoke) tests tend to use virtual resources that are pre-configured, while later (Integration) test tend to run on representative hardware or clean VMs, with the software built from scratch.

You will also note that we did not call out *Regression* tests in this simple taxonomy, but our view is that Regression tests are designed to ensure that a bug is not re-introduced into the code once it has been identified and fixed, meaning it is a common *source* of new tests that can be added to Unit, Smoke, Integration, Performance, or Soak tests. Most tests, in practice, are Regression tests, independent of where they run in the CI/CD pipeline.

4.2.2 *Testing Framework*

With respect to a testing framework, Figure 20 shows an illustrative example drawn from Aether. Specifics will vary substantially, depending on the kind of functionality you need to test. In Aether, the relevant components are shown on the right—rearranged to highlight top-down dependencies between subsystems—with the corresponding test-automation tool shown on the left. Think of each of these as a framework for a domain-specific class of tests (e.g., NG40 puts a 5G workload on SD-Core and SD-RAN, while TestVectors injects packet traffic into the switches).

Some of the frameworks shown in Figure 20 were co-developed with the corresponding software component. This is true of TestVectors and TestON, which put customized workloads on Stratum (SwitchOS) and ONOS (NetworkOS), respectively. Both are open source, and hence available to be perused for insights into the challenges of building a testing framework. In contrast, NG40 is a close source, proprietary framework for emulating 3GPP-compliant cellular network traffic.

Selenium and Robot are the most general of the five examples. Each is an open source project with an active developer community. Selenium is a tool for automating the testing of web applications,

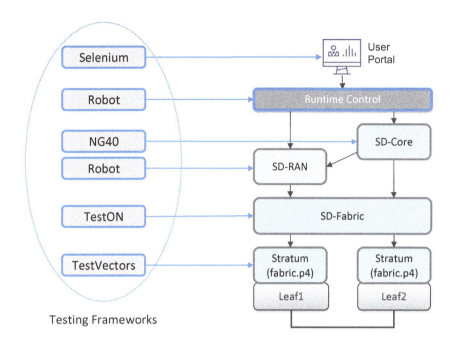

Figure 20: Example Testing Frameworks used in Aether.

while Robot is a more general tool for generating requests to any well-defined interface. Both systems are frameworks in the sense that developers can write extensions, libraries, drivers, and plugins to test specific features of the User Portal and the Runtime API, respectively.[11] They both illustrate the purpose of a testing framework, which is to provide a means to (1) automate the execution of a range of tests; (2) collect and archive the resulting test results; and (3) evaluate and analyze the test results. In addition, is it necessary for such frameworks to be scalable when they are used to test systems that are themselves intended to be scalable, as is the case for cloud services.

Finally, as discussed in the previous subsection, each of these testing frameworks requires a set of resources. These resources are for running both the suite of tests (which generates workload) and the subsystem(s) being tested. For the latter, reproducing a full replica of the target cluster for every development team is ideal, but it is more cost-effective to implement virtual environments that can be instantiated on-demand in a cloud. Fortunately, because the software being

[11] Selenium is actually available as a library that can be called from within the Robot framework, which makes sense when you consider that a web GUI invokes HTTP operations on a set of HTML-defined elements, such as textboxes, buttons, drop-down menus, and so on.

developed is containerized and Kubernetes can run in a VM, virtual testing environments are straightforward to support. This means dedicated hardware can be reserved for less-frequent (e.g., daily) integration tests.

4.3 Continuous Integration

The Continuous Integration (CI) half of Lifecycle Management is all about translating source code checked in by developers into a deployable set of Docker Images. As discussed in the previous section, this is largely an exercise in running a set of tests against the code—first to test if it is ready to be integrated and then to test if it was successfully integrated—where the integration itself is entirely carried out according to a declarative specification. This is the value proposition of the microservices architecture: each of the components is developed independently, packaged as a container (Docker), and then deployed and interconnected by a container management system (Kubernetes) according to a declarative integration plan (Helm).

But this story overlooks a few important details that we now discuss, in part by filling in some specific mechanisms.

4.3.1 Code Repositories

Code Repositories (of which GitHub and Gerrit are two examples), typically provide a means to tentatively submit a patch set, triggering a set of static checks (e.g., passes linter, license, and CLA checks), and giving code reviewers a chance to inspect and comment on the code. This mechanism also provides a means to trigger the build-integrate-test processes discussed next. Once all such checks complete to the satisfaction of the engineers responsible for the affected modules, the patch set is merged. This is all part of the well-understood software development process, and so we do not discuss it further. The important takeaway for our purposes is that there is a well-defined interface between code repositories and subsequent stages of the CI/CD pipeline.

4.3.2 Build-Integrate-Test

The heart of the CI pipeline is a mechanism for executing a set of processes that (a) build the component(s) impacted by a given patch set, (b) integrate the resulting executable images (e.g, binaries) with other images to construct larger subsystems, (c) run a set of tests against those integrated subsystems and post the results, and (d) optionally publish new deployment artifacts (e.g, Docker images) to the downstream image repository. This last step happens only after the patch set has been accepted and merged into the repo (which also triggers the *Build* stage in Figure 18 to run). Importantly, the manner in which images are built and integrated for testing is exactly the same as the way they are built and integrated for deployment. The design principle is that there are no special cases, just different "off-ramps" for the end-to-end CI/CD pipeline.

There is no topic on which developers have stronger opinions than the merits (and flaws) of different build tools. Old-school C coders raised on Unix prefer Make. Google developed Bazel, and made it available as open source. The Apache Foundation released Maven, which evolved into Gradle. We prefer to not pick sides in this un-winnable debate, but instead acknowledge that different teams will pick different build tools for their individual projects (which we've been referring to in generic terms as subsystems), and we will employ a simple second-level tool to integrate the output of all those sophisticated first-level tools. Our choice for the second-level mechanism is Jenkins, a job automation tool that system admins have been using for years, but which has recently been adapted and extended to automate CI/CD pipelines.

At a high level, Jenkins is little more than a mechanism that executes a script, called a *job*, in response to some *trigger*. Like many of the tools described in this book, Jenkins has a graphical dashboard that can be used to create, execute, and view the results of a set of jobs, but this is mostly useful for simple examples. Because Jenkins plays a central role in our CI pipeline, it is managed like all the other components we are building—via a collection of declarative specifi-

Further Reading:
Jenkins (`https://www.jenkins.io/doc/`).

cation files that are checked into a repo. The question, then, is exactly what do we specify?

Jenkins provides a scripting language, called *Groovy*, that can be used to define a *Pipeline* consisting of a sequence of *Stages*. Each stage executes some task and tests whether it succeeded or failed. In principle then, you could define a single CI/CD pipeline for the entire system. It would start with "Build" stage, followed by a "Test" stage, and then conditional upon success, conclude with a "Deliver" stage. But this approach doesn't take into account the loose coupling of all the components that go into building a cloud. Instead, what happens in practice is that Jenkins is used more narrowly to (1) build and test individual components, both before and after they are merged into the code repository; (2) integrate and test various combinations of components, for example, on a nightly basis; and (3) under limited conditions, push the artifact that has just been built (e.g., a Docker Image) to the Image Repo.

This is a non-trivial undertaking, and so Jenkins supports tooling to help construct jobs. Specifically, *Jenkins Job Builder (JJB)* processes declarative YAML files that "parameterize" the Pipeline definitions written in Groovy, producing the set of jobs that Jenkins then runs. Among other things, these YAML files specify the triggers—such as a patch being checked into the code repo—that launch the pipeline.

Exactly how developers use JJB is an engineering detail, but in Aether, the approach is for each major component to define three or four different Groovy-based pipelines, each of which you can think of as corresponding to one of the top-level stages in the overall CI/CD pipeline shown in Figure 18. That is, one Groovy pipeline corresponds to pre-merge build and test, one for post-merge build and test, one for integrate and test, and one for publish artifact. Each major component also defines a collection of YAML files that link component-specific triggers to one of the pipelines, along with the associated set of parameters for that pipeline. The number of YAML files (and hence triggers) varies from component to component, but one common example is a specification to publish a new Docker image, triggered by a change to a VERSION file stored in the code repo. (We'll see why in Section 4.5.)

As an illustrative example, the following is from a Groovy script that defines the pipeline for testing the Aether API, which, as we'll see in the next chapter, is auto-generated by the Runtime Control subsystem. We're interested in the general form of the pipeline, so omit most of the details, but it should be clear from the example what each stage does. (Recall that Kind is Kubernetes in Docker.) The one stage fully depicted in the example invokes the Robot testing framework introduced in Section 4.2.2, with each invocation exercising a different feature of the API. (To improve readability, the example does not show the *output*, *logging*, and *report* arguments to Robot, which collect the results.)

```
pipeline {
...
    stages {
        stage("Cleanup"){
            ...
        }
        stage("Install Kind"){
            ...
        }
        stage("Clone Test Repo"){
            ...
        }
        stage("Setup Virtual Environment"){
            ...
        }
        stage("Generate API Test Framework and API Tests"){
            ...
        }
        stage("Run API Tests"){
            steps {
                sh """
                    mkdir -p /tmp/robotlogs
                    cd ${WORKSPACE}/api-tests
                    source ast-venv/bin/activate; set -u;
                    robot ${WORKSPACE}/api-tests/ap_list.robot || true
                    robot ${WORKSPACE}/api-tests/application.robot || true
                    robot ${WORKSPACE}/api-tests/connectivity_service.robot || true
```

```
                    robot ${WORKSPACE}/api-tests/device_group.robot || true
                    robot ${WORKSPACE}/api-tests/enterprise.robot || true
                    robot ${WORKSPACE}/api-tests/ip_domain.robot || true
                    robot ${WORKSPACE}/api-tests/site.robot || true
                    robot ${WORKSPACE}/api-tests/template.robot || true
                    robot ${WORKSPACE}/api-tests/traffic_class.robot || true
                    robot ${WORKSPACE}/api-tests/upf.robot || true
                    robot ${WORKSPACE}/api-tests/vcs.robot || true
                """
            }
        }
    }
  ...
}
```

One thing to notice is that this is another example of a tool using
generic terminology in a specific way, which does not align with our
conceptual use. Each conceptual *stage* in Figure 18 is implemented
by one or more Groovy-defined *pipelines*, each of which consists of a
sequence of Groovy-defined *stages*. And as we can see in this example,
these Groovy stages are quite low-level.

This particular pipeline is part of the post-build QA testing stage
shown in Figure 18, and so is invoked by a time-based trigger. The following snippet of YAML is an example of a job template that specifies
such a trigger. Note that the value of the name attribute is what you
would see if you looked at the set of jobs in the Jenkins dashboard.

```
- job-template:
    id: aether-api-tests
    name: 'aether-api-{api-version}-tests-{release-version}'
    project-type: pipeline
    pipeline-file: 'aether-api-tests.groovy'
    ...
    triggers:
      - timed: |
          TZ=America/Los_Angeles
          H {time} * * *
...
```

To complete the picture, the follow code snippet from another YAML file shows how a repo-based trigger is specified. This example executes a different pipeline (not shown), and corresponds to a pre-merge test that runs when a developer submits a candidate patch set.

```
- job-template:
    id: 'aether-patchset'
    name: 'aether-verify-{project}{suffix}'
    project-type: pipeline
    pipeline-script: 'aether-test.groovy'
    ...
    triggers:
      - gerrit:
          server-name: '{gerrit-server-name}'
          dependency-jobs: '{dependency-jobs}'
          trigger-on:
            - patchset-created-event:
                exclude-drafts: true
                exclude-trivial-rebase: false
                exclude-no-code-change: true
            - draft-published-event
            - comment-added-contains-event:
                comment-contains-value: '(?i)^.*recheck$'
...
```

Balancing DIY Tools with Cloud Services

Aether uses Jenkins as its CI tool, but another popular option is GitHub Actions. This is a feature of GitHub (the cloud service, not to be confused with the software tool Git) that augments a repo with a set of workflows that can be executed every time a patch is submitted. In this setting, a workflow is roughly analogous to a Groovy pipeline.

GitHub actions are especially convenient for open source projects because they include spinning up a container in which the workflow runs (for free, but with limits). A mixed strategy would be to run simple GitHub Actions for unit and smoke tests when code is checked in, but then use Jenkins to manage complex integration tests that require additional testing resources (e.g., a full QA cluster).

> *GitHub Actions are not unique. Many of the open source options described in this book are paired with a cloud service counterpart. The key consideration is how much you want to depend on a service someone else provides versus depending entirely on services you install and manage yourself. The former can be easier, but comes with the risk that the provider changes (or discontinues) the service. The same can be said of open source projects, but having access to source code gives you more control over your fate.*

The important takeaway from this discussion is that there is no single or global CI job. There are many per-component jobs that independently publish deployable artifacts when conditions dictate. Those conditions include: (1) the component passes the required tests, and (2) the component's version indicates whether or not a new artifact is warranted. We have already talked about the testing strategy in Section 4.2 and we describe the versioning strategy in Section 4.5. These two concerns are at the heart of realizing a sound approach to Continuous Integration. The tooling—in our case Jenkins—is just a means to that end.

4.4 Continuous Deployment

We are now ready to act on the configuration specs checked into the Config Repo, which includes both the set of Terraform Templates that specify the underlying infrastructure (we've been calling this the cloud platform) and the set of Helm Charts that specify the collection of microservices (sometimes called applications) that are to be deployed on that infrastructure. We discussed Terraform in Chapter 3: it's the agent that actually "acts on" the infrastructure-related forms. For its counterpart on the application side Aether uses an open source project called Fleet.

Figure 21 shows the big picture we are working towards. Note that both Fleet and Terraform depend on the Provisioning API exported by each backend cloud, although roughly speaking, Terraform invokes the "manage Kubernetes" aspects of those APIs, and Fleet invokes the "use Kubernetes" aspects of those APIs. Consider each in turn.

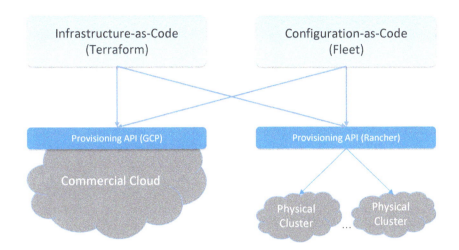

Figure 21: Relationship between the main CD agents (Terraform and Fleet) and the backend Kubernetes clusters.

The Terraform side of Figure 21 is responsible for deploying (and configuring) the latest platform level software. For example, if the operator wants to add a server (or VM) to a given cluster, upgrade the version of Kubernetes, or change the CNI plug-in Kubernetes uses, the desired configuration is specified in the Terraform config files. (Recall that Terraform computes the delta between the existing and desired state, and executes the calls required to bring the former in line with the latter.) Anytime new hardware is added to an existing cluster, the corresponding Terraform file is modified accordingly and checked into the Config Repo, triggering the deployment job. We do not reiterate the mechanistic aspect of how platform deployments are triggered, but it uses exactly the same set of Jenkins machinery described in Section 4.3.2, except now watching for changes to Terraform Forms checked into the Config Repo.

The Fleet side of Figure 21 is responsible for installing the collection of microservices that are to run on each cluster. These microservices, organized as one or more applications, are specified by Helm Charts. If we were trying to deploy a single Chart on just one one Kubernetes cluster, then we'd be done: Helm is exactly the right tool to carry out that task. The value of Fleet is that it scales up that process, helping us manage the deployment of multiple charts across multiple clusters. (Fleet is a spin-off from Rancher, but is an independent mechanism.)

Further Reading:
Fleet: GitOps at Scale
(`https://fleet.rancher.io/`).

Fleet defines three concepts that are relevant to our discussion. The first is a *Bundle*, which defines the fundamental unit of what gets deployed. In our case, a Bundle is equivalent to a set of one or more Helm Charts. The second is a *Cluster Group*, which identifies a set of Kubernetes clusters that are to be treated in an equivalent way. In our case, the set of all clusters labeled Production could be treated as one such a group, and all clusters labeled Staging could be treated as another such group. (Here, we are talking about the env label assigned to each cluster in its Terraform spec, as illustrated in the examples shown in Section 3.2.) The third is a *GitRepo*, which is a repository to watch for changes to bundle artifacts. In our case, new Helm Charts are checked into the Config Repo (but as indicated at the beginning of this chapter, there is likely a dedicated "Helm Repo" in practice).

Understanding Fleet is then straightforward. It provides a way to define associations between Bundles, Cluster Groups, and GitRepos, such that whenever an updated Helm chart is checked into a GitRepo, all Bundles that contain that chart are (re-)deployed on all associated Cluster Groups. That is to say, Fleet can be viewed as the mechanism that implements the *Deployment Gate* shown in Figure 18, although other factors can also be taken into account (e.g., not starting a rollout at 5pm on a Friday afternoon). The next section describes a versioning strategy that can be overlaid on this mechanism to control what features get deployed when.

Implementation Details Matter

We are purposely not doing a deep-dive into the individual tools that are assembled into the Lifecycle Management subsystem, but details do often matter. Our experience with Fleet offers a good example. As a careful reader may have noticed, we could have used Jenkins to trigger Fleet to deploy an upgraded application, similar to how we do with Terraform. Instead, we decided to use Fleet's internal triggering mechanism because of the convenience of its Bundle and Cluster Group abstractions.

After Fleet came online as the Deployment mechanism, developers noticed that the code repo became extremely sluggish. It turned out this is because Fleet polls the specified GitRepos to detect changes to the watched Bundles, and the polling was so frequent it overloaded the repo. A "polling-frequency" parameter change improved the situation, but led people to wonder why Jenkins' trigger mechanism hadn't caused the same problem. The answer is that Jenkins is better integrated with the repo, with a GitHub webhook pushing event notifications to Jenkins when a file check-in actually occurs. There is no polling. (Polling can also be disabled in Fleet, in favor of webhooks, but polling is the default.)

This focus on Fleet as the agent triggering the execution of Helm Charts should not distract from the central role of the charts themselves. They are the centerpiece of how we specify service deployments. They identify the interconnected set of microservices to be deployed, and as we'll see in the next section, are the ultimate arbitrator of the version of each of those microservices. Later chapters will also describe how these charts sometimes specify a Kubernetes *Operator* that is to run when a microservice is deployed, configuring the newly started microservice in some component-specific way. Finally, Helm Charts can specify the resources (e.g., processor cores) each microservice is permitted to consume, including both minimal thresholds and upper limits. Of course, all of this is possible only because Kubernetes supports the corresponding API calls, and enforces resource usage accordingly.

Note that this last point about resource allocation shines a light on a fundamental characteristic of the kind of edge/hybrid clouds we're focused on: they are typically resource constrained, as opposed to offering the seemingly infinite resources of a datacenter-based elastic cloud. As a consequence, provisioning and lifecycle management are implicitly linked by the analysis used to decide (1) what services we want to deploy, (2) how many resources those services require, and (3) how the available resources are to be shared among the curated set of services.

4.5 Versioning Strategy

The CI/CD toolchain introduced in this chapter works only when applied in concert with an end-to-end versioning strategy, ensuring that the right combination of source modules get integrated, and later, the right combination of images gets deployed. Remember, the high-level challenge is to manage the set of features that our cloud supports, which is another way of saying that everything hinges on how we version those features.

Our starting point is to adopt the widely-accepted practice of *Semantic Versioning*, where each component is assigned a three-part version number *MAJOR.MINOR.PATCH* (e.g., 3.2.4), where the *MAJOR* version increments whenever you make an incompatible API change, the *MINOR* version increments when you add functionality in a backward-compatible way, and the *PATCH* corresponds to a backward-compatible bug fix.

The following sketches one possible interplay between versioning and the CI/CD toolchain, keeping in mind there are different approaches to the problem. We break the sequence down to the three main phases of the software lifecycle:

Further Reading:
Semantic Versioning 2.0.0
(https://semver.org).

Development Time

- Every patch checked into a source code repo includes an up-to-date semantic version number in a VERSION file in the repository. Note that every *patch* does not necessarily equal every *commit*, as it is not uncommon to make multiple changes to an "in development" version, sometimes denoted 3.2.4-dev, for example. This VERSION file is used by developers to keep track of the current version number, but as we saw in Section 4.3.2, it also serves as a trigger for a Jenkins job that potentially publishes a new Docker or Helm artifact.

- The commit that does correspond to a finalized patch is also tagged (in the repo) with the corresponding semantic version number. In Git, this tag is bound to a hash that unambiguously identifies the commit, making it the authoritative way of binding a version number to a particular instance of the source code.

- For repos that correspond to microservices, the repo also has a Dockerfile that gives the recipe for building a Docker image from that (and other) software module(s).

Integration Time

- The CI toolchain does a sanity check on each component's version number, ensuring it doesn't regress, and when it sees a new number for a microservice, builds a new image and uploads it to the image repo. By convention, this image includes the corresponding source code version number in the unique name assigned to the image.

Deployment Time

- The CD toolchain instantiates the set of Docker Images, as specified by name in one or more Helm Charts. Since these image names include the semantic version number, by convention, we know the corresponding software version being deployed.

- Each Helm Chart is also checked into a repository, and hence, has its own version number. Each time a Helm Chart changes, because the version of a constituent Docker Image changes, the chart's version number also changes.

- Helm Charts can be organized hierarchically, that is, with one Chart including one or more other Charts (each with their own version number), with the version of the root Chart effectively identifying the version of the system as a whole being deployed.

Note that a commit of a new version of the root Helm Chart could be taken as the signal to the CD half of the pipeline—as denoted by the the *"Deployment Gate"* in Figure 18—that the combination of modules (features) is now deployment-ready. Of course, other factors can also be taken into consideration, such as time of day as noted above.

While some of the *Source Code → Docker Image → Kubernetes Container* relationships just outlined can be codified in the toolchain, at least at the level of automated sanity tests that catch obvious mistakes, responsibility ultimately falls to the developers checking in source code and the operators checking in configuration code; they must correctly specify the versions they intend. Having a simple and clear versioning strategy is a prerequisite for doing that job.

Finally, because versioning is inherently related to APIs, with the *MAJOR* version number incremented whenever the API changes in a non-backward-compatible way, developers are responsible for ensuring their software is able to correctly consume any APIs they depend on. Doing so becomes problematic when there is persistent state involved, by which we mean state that must be preserved across multiple versions of the software that accesses it. This is a problem that all operational systems that run continuously have to deal with, and typically requires a *data migration* strategy. Solving this problem in a general way for application-level state is beyond the scope of this book, but solving it for the cloud management system (which has its own persistent state) is a topic we take up in the next chapter.

4.6 Managing Secrets

The discussion up to this point has glossed over one important detail, which is how secrets are managed. These include, for example, the credentials Terraform needs to access remote services like GCP, as well as the keys used to secure communication among microservices within an edge cluster. Such secrets are effectively part of the hybrid cloud's configuration state, which would imply they are stored in the Config Repo, like all other Configuration-as-Code artifacts. But repositories are typically not designed to be secure, which is problematic.

At a high level, the solution is straightforward. The various secrets required to operate a secure system are encrypted, and only the encrypted versions are checked into the Config Repo. This reduces the problem to worrying about just one secret, but effectively kicks the can down the road. How, then, do we manage (both protect and distribute) the secret needed to decrypt the secrets? Fortunately, there are mechanisms available to help solve that problem. Aether, for example, uses two different approaches, each with its own strengths and weaknesses.

One approach is exemplified by the git-crypt tool, which closely matches the high-level summary outlined in the previous paragraph. In this case, the "central processing loop" of the CI/CD mechanism—which corresponds to Jenkins in Aether—is the trusted entity responsible for decrypting the component-specific secrets and passing them along to various components at deployment time. This "pass along" step is typically implemented using the Kubernetes *Secrets* mechanism, which is an encrypted channel for sending configuration state to microservices (i.e., it is similar to *ConfigMaps*). This mechanism should not be confused with *SealedSecrets* (discussed next) because it does not, by itself, address the larger issue we're discussing here, which is how secrets are managed **outside** a running cluster.

This approach has the advantage of being general because it makes few assumptions and works for all secrets and components. But it comes with the downside of investing significant trust in Jenkins, or more to the point, in the practices the DevOps team adopts for how they use Jenkins.

The second approach is exemplified by Kubernetes' *SealedSecrets* mechanism. The idea is to trust a process running within the Kubernetes cluster (technically, this process is known as a Controller) to manage secrets on behalf of all the other Kubernetes-hosted microservices. At runtime, this process creates a Private/Public key pair, and makes the Public key available to the CI/CD toolchain. The Private key is restricted to the SealedSecrets Controller, and is referred to as the *sealing key*. Without stepping through the details of the full protocol, the Public key is used in combination with a randomly-generated symmetric key to encrypt all the secrets that need to be stored in the Config Repo, and later (at deployment time), the individual microservices ask the SealedSecrets Controller to use its sealing key to help them unlock those secrets.

While this approach is less general than the first (i.e., it is specific to protecting secrets within a Kubernetes cluster), it has the advantage of taking humans out of the loop, with the sealing key being programmatically generated at runtime. One complication, however, is that it is generally preferable for that secret to be written to persistentstorage, to protect against having to restart the SealedSecrets Controller. This potentially opens up an attack surface that needs to be protected.

Further Reading:
git-crypt (`https://github.com/AGWA/git-crypt/blob/master/README.md`).

"Sealed Secrets" for Kubernetes (`https://github.com/bitnami-labs/sealed-secrets`).

4.7 *What about GitOps?*

The CI/CD pipeline described in this chapter is consistent with Gi-tOps, an approach to DevOps designed around the idea of *Configuration-as-Code*—making the code repo the single source of truth for building and deploying a cloud native system. The approach is premised on first making all configuration state declarative (e.g, specified in Helm Charts and Terraform Templates), and then treating this repo as the single source of truth for building and deploying a cloud native system. It doesn't matter if you patch a Python file or update a config file, the repo triggers the CI/CD pipeline as described in this chapter.

While the approach described in this chapter is based on the Gi-tOps model, there are three considerations that mean GitOps is not the end of the story. All hinge on the question of whether **all** state needed to operate a cloud native system can be managed **entirely** with a repository-based mechanism.

The first consideration is that we need to acknowledge the difference between people who develop software and people who build and operate systems using that software. DevOps (in its simplest formulation) implies there should be no distinction. In practice, developers are often far removed from operators, or more to the point, they are far removed from design decisions about exactly how others will end up using their software. For example, software is usually implemented with a particular set of use cases in mind, but it is later integrated with other software to build entirely new cloud apps that have their own set of abstractions and features, and correspondingly, their own collection of configuration state. This is true for Aether, where the SD-Core subsystem, for example, was originally implemented for use in global cellular networks, but is being repurposed to support private 4G/5G in enterprises.

While it is true such state could be managed in a Git repository, the idea of configuration management by pull request is overly simplistic. There are both low-level (implementation-centric) and high-level (application-centric) variables; in other words, it is common to have one or more layers of abstraction running on top of the base software. In the limit, it may even be an end-user (e.g., an enterprise user in Aether) who wants to change this state, which implies fine-grained access control is likely a requirement. None of this disqualifies GitOps as a way to manage such state, but it does raise the possibility that not all state is created equal—that there is a range of configuration state variables being accessed at different times by different people with different skill sets, and most importantly, needing different levels of privilege.

The second consideration has to do with where configuration state originates. For example, consider the addresses assigned to the servers assembled in a cluster, which might originate in an organization's inventory system. Or in another example specific to Aether, it is necessary to call a remote *Spectrum Access Service (SAS)* to learn how to configure the radio settings for the small cells that have been deployed. Naively, you might think that's a variable you could pull out of a YAML file stored in a Git repository. In general, systems often have to deal with multiple—sometimes external—sources of configuration state, and knowing which copy is authoritative and which is derivative is problematic. There is no single right answer, but situations like this raise the possibility that the authoritative copy of configuration state needs to be maintained apart from any single use of that state.

The third consideration is how frequently this state changes, and hence, potentially triggers restarting or possibly even re-deploying a set of containers. Doing so certainly makes sense for "set once" configuration parameters, but what about "runtime settable" control variables? What is the most cost-effective way to update system parameters that have the potential to change frequently? Again, this raises the possibility that not all state is created equal, and that there is a continuum of configuration state variables.

These three considerations point to there being a distinction between build-time configuration state and runtime control state, the topic of the next chapter. We emphasize, however, that the question of how to manage such state does not have a single correct answer; drawing a crisp line between "configuration" and "control" is notoriously difficult. Both the repo-based mechanism championed by GitOps and runtime control alternatives described in the next chapter provide value, and it is a question of which is the better match for any given piece of information that needs to be maintained for a cloud to operate properly.

Chapter 5: Runtime Control

Runtime Control provides an API by which various principals, such as end-users, enterprise admins, and cloud operators, can make changes to a running system, by specifying new values for one or more runtime parameters.

Using Aether's 5G connectivity service as an example, suppose an enterprise admin wants to change the *Quality-of-Service* for a group of mobile devices. Aether defines a *Device Group* abstraction so that related devices can be configured together. The admin can then modify the *Maximum Uplink Bandwidth* or *Maximum Downlink Bandwidth*, or even select a different *Traffic Class* for the group. Similarly, imagine an operator wants to add a new *Mission-Critical* option to the existing set of *Traffic Classes* that devices can adopt. Without worrying about the exact syntax of the API call(s) for these operations, the Runtime Control subsystem needs to:

1. Authenticate the principal wanting to perform the operation.

2. Determine if that principal has sufficient privilege to carry out the operation.

3. Push the new parameter setting(s) to one or more backend components.

4. Record the specified parameter setting(s), so the new value(s) persist.

In this example, *Device Group* and *Traffic Class* are abstract objects being operated upon, and while these objects must be understood by

Runtime Control, making changes to them might involve invoking low-level control operations on multiple subsystems, such as the SD-RAN (which is responsible for QoS in the RAN), the SD-Fabric (which is responsible for QoS through the switching fabric), SD-Core UP (which is responsible for QoS in the mobile core user plane), and SD-Core CP (which is responsible for QoS in the mobile core control plane).

In short, Runtime Control defines an abstraction layer on top of a collection of backend components, effectively turning them into externally visible (and controllable) cloud services. Sometimes a single backend component implements the entirety of a service, in which case Runtime Control may add little more than a Triple-A layer. But for a cloud constructed from a collection of disaggregated components, Runtime Control is where we define an API that logically integrates those components into a unified and coherent set of abstract services. It is also an opportunity to "raise the level of abstraction" for the underlying subsystems and hiding implementation details.

Note that because of its role assembling an end-to-end service across a set of backend components, the Runtime Control mechanism described in this chapter is similar to a *Service Orchestrator* that chains together a collection of VNFs in a Telco network. Either term could be used here, but we have elected to use "Runtime Control" to emphasize the temporal aspect of the problem, especially its relationship to lifecycle management. It is also the case that "orchestration" is a loaded term with different connotations in different contexts. In a Cloud setting it implies assembling virtual resources, while in a Telco setting it implies assembling virtual functions. As is often the case in complex systems (especially when they promote competing business models), the higher you go in the stack, the less consensus there is about terminology.

Whatever you call the mechanism, defining a set of abstractions and the corresponding API is a challenging job. Having the appropriate tools helps to focus on the creative part of that task, but by no means eliminates it. The challenge is partly a matter of judgment about what should be visible to users and what should be a hidden implementation detail, and partly about dealing with conflicting/conflated concepts and terminology. We'll see a full example in Section 5.3, but to illustrate the difficulty, consider how Aether refers to principals in its 5G connectivity service. If we were to borrow terminology directly from the Telcos, then we'd refer to someone that uses a mobile device as a *subscriber*, implying an account and a collection of settings for the service delivered to that device. And in fact, subscriber is a central object within the SD-Core implementation. But Aether is designed to support enterprise deployments of 5G, and to that end, defines a *user* to be a principal that accesses the API or GUI portal with some prescribed level of privilege. There is not necessarily a one-to-one relationship between users and Core-defined subscribers, and more importantly, not all devices have subscribers; a concrete example would be IoT devices that are not typically associated with a particular person.

5.1 Design Overview

At a high level, the purpose of Runtime Control is to offer an API that various stakeholders can use to configure and control cloud services. In doing so, Runtime Control must:

- Support new end-to-end abstractions that may cross multiple back-end subsystems.

- Associate control and configuration state with those abstractions.

- Support *versioning* of this configuration state, so changes can be rolled back as necessary, and an audit history may be retrieved of previous configurations.

- Adopt best practices of *performance*, *high availability*, *reliability*, and *security* in how this abstraction layer is implemented.

- Support *Role-Based Access Controls (RBAC)*, so that different principals have different visibility into and control over the underlying abstract objects.

- Be extensible, and so able to incorporate new services and new abstractions for existing services over time.

Central to this role is the requirement that Runtime Control be able to represent a set of abstract objects, which is to say, it implements a *data model*. While there are several viable options for the specification language used to represent the data model, for Runtime Control Aether uses YANG. This is for three reasons. First, YANG is a rich language for data modeling, with support for strong validation of the data stored in the models and the ability to define relations between objects. Second, it is agnostic as to how the data is stored (i.e., not directly tied to SQL/RDBMS or NoSQL paradigms), giving us a generous set of engineering options. Finally, YANG is widely used for this purpose, meaning there is a robust collection of YANG-based tools that we can build upon.

Further Reading:
YANG - A Data Modeling Language for the Network Configuration Protocol. RFC 6020. October 2010.

Web Frameworks

The role Runtime Control plays in operationalizing a cloud is similar to the role a Web Framework plays in operationalizing a web service. If you start with the assumption that certain classes of users will interact with your system (in our case, an edge cloud) via a GUI, then either you write that GUI in a language like PHP (as early web developers did), our you take advantage of a framework like Django or Ruby on Rails. What such frameworks provide is a way to define a set of user-friendly abstractions (these are called Models), a means to visualize those abstractions in a GUI (these are called Views), and a means to affect change on collection of backend systems based on user input (these are called Controllers). It is not an accident that Model-View-Controller (MVP) is a well-understood design paradigm.

The Runtime Control system described in this chapter adopts a similar approach, but instead of defining the models in Python (as with Django) or Ruby (as with Ruby on Rails), we define models using a declarative language (YANG) which is in turn used to generate a programmatic API. This API can then be invoked from (1) a GUI, which is itself typically built using another framework, such as AngularJS; (2) a CLI; or (3) a closed-loop control program. There are other differences—for example, Adaptors (a kind of Controller) use gNMI as a standard interface for controlling backend compo-

nents, and persistent state is stored in a key-value store instead of a SQL DB—but the biggest difference is the use of a declarative rather than an imperative language to define models.

With this background, Figure 22 shows the internal structure of Runtime Control for Aether, which has *x-config*—a microservice that maintains a set of YANG models—at its core.[12] x-config, in turn, uses Atomix (a key-value store microservice), to make configuration state persistent. Because x-config was originally designed to manage configuration state for devices, it uses gNMI as its southbound interface to communicate configuration changes to devices (or in our case, software services). An Adaptor has to be written for any service/device that does not support gNMI natively. These adaptors are shown as part of Runtime Control in Figure 22, but it is equally correct to view each adaptor as part of the backend component, responsible for making that component management-ready. Finally, Runtime Control includes a Workflow Engine that is responsible for executing multi-step operations on the data model. This happens, for example, when a change to one model triggers some action on another model. Each of these components are described in more detail in the next section.

The Runtime Control API is auto-generated from the YANG-based data model, and as shown in Figure 22, supports two portals and a set of closed-loop control applications. There is also a CLI (not shown). This API provides a single entry-point for **all** control information that can be read or written in Aether, and as a consequence, Runtime Control can also mediate access to the other subsystems of the Control and Management Platform (not just the subsystems shown in Figure 22).

This situation is illustrated in Figure 23, where the key takeaways are that (1) we want RBAC and auditing for all operations; (2) we want a single source of authoritative configuration state; and (3) we want to grant limited (fine-grained) access to management functions to arbitrary principals rather than assume only a single privileged class of operators. Of course, the private APIs of the underlying subsystems still exist, and operators can directly use them. This can be especially useful when diagnosing problems, but for the three rea-

[12] x-config is a general-purpose, model-agnostic tool. In AMP, it manages YANG models for cloud services, but it is also used by SD-Fabric to manage YANG models for a set of network switches and by SD-RAN to manage YANG models for a set of RAN elements. This means multiple instances of the x-config microservice run in a given Aether edge cluster.

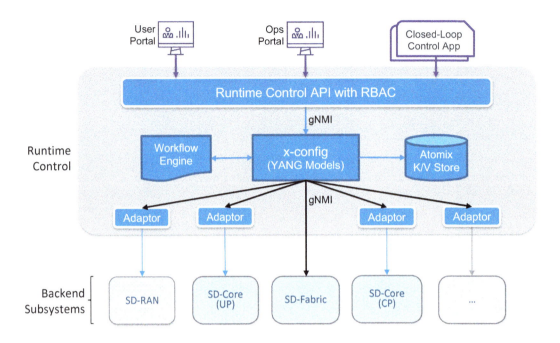

Figure 22: Internal structure of Runtime Control, and its relationship to backend subsystems (below) and user portals/apps (above).

sons given above, there is a strong argument in favor of mediating all control activity using the Runtime Control API.

This discussion is related to the "What About GitOps?" question raised at the end of Chapter 4. We return to that same question at the end of this chapter, but to set the stage, we now have the option of Runtime Control maintaining authoritative configuration and control state for the system in its key-value store. This raises the question of how to "share ownership" of configuration state with the repositories that implement Lifecycle Management.

One option is to decide on a case-by-case basis: Runtime Control maintains authoritative state for some parameters and the Config Repo maintains authoritative state for other parameters. We just need to be clear about which is which, so each backend component knows which "configuration path" it needs to be responsive to. Then, for any repo-maintained state for which we want Runtime Control to mediate access (e.g., to provide fine-grained access for a more expansive set of principals), we need to be careful about the consequences of any backdoor (direct) changes to that repo-maintained state, for example, by storing only a cached copy of that state in Runtime Control's key-value store (as an optimization).

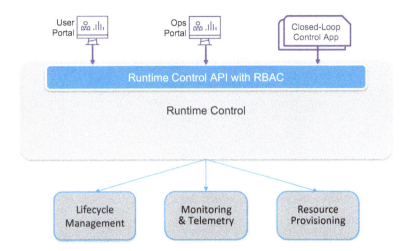

Figure 23: Runtime Control also mediates access to the other Management Services.

Another aspect of Figure 23 worth noting is that, while Runtime Control mediates all control-related activity, it is not in the "data path" for the subsystems it controls. This means, for example, that monitoring data returned by the Monitoring & Telemetry subsystem does not pass through Runtime Control; it is delivered directly to dashboards and applications running on top of the API. Runtime Control is only involved in authorizing access to such data. It is also the case that Runtime Control and the Monitoring subsystem have their own, independent data stores: it is the Atomix key-value store for Runtime Control and a Time-Series DB for Monitoring (as discussed in more detail in Chapter 6).

In summary, the value of a unified Runtime Control API is best illustrated by the ability to implement closed-loop control applications (and other dashboards) that "read" data collected by the Monitoring subsystem; perform some kind of analysis on that data, possibly resulting in a decision to take corrective action; and then "write" new control directives, which x-config passes along to some combination of SD-RAN, SD-Core, and SD-Fabric, or sometimes even to the Lifecycle Management subsystem. (We'll see an example of the latter in

Section 5.3.) This closed-loop scenario is depicted in Figure 24, which gives a different perspective by showing the Monitoring subsystem as a "peer" of Runtime Control (rather than below it), although both perspectives are valid.

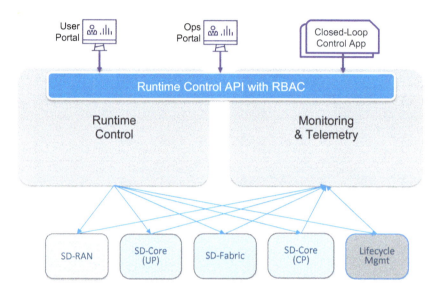

Figure 24: Another perspective of Runtime Control, illustrating the value of a unified API that supports closed-loop control applications.

5.2 Implementation Details

This section describes each of the components in Runtime Control, focusing on the role each plays in cloud management.

5.2.1 Models & State

x-config is the core of the Runtime Control. Its job is to store and version configuration data. Configuration is pushed to x-config through its northbound gNMI interface, stored in a persistent key-value store, and pushed to backend subsystems using a southbound gNMI interface.

A collection of YANG-based models define the schema for this configuration state. These models are loaded into x-config, and collectively define the data model for all the configuration and control state that Runtime Control is responsible for. As an example, the data model (schema) for Aether is sketched in Section 5.3, but another example would be the set of OpenConfig models used to manage network devices.

There are four important aspects of this mechanism:

Further Reading:
OpenConfig (`https://www.openconfig.net/`).

- **Persistent Store:** Atomix is the cloud native key-value store used to persist data in x-config. Atomix supports a distributed map abstraction, which implements the Raft consensus algorithm to achieve fault-tolerance and scalable performance. x-config writes data to and reads data from Atomix using a simple GET/PUT interface common to NoSQL databases.

- **Loading Models:** Models are loaded using *Model Plugins*. x-config communicates via a gRPC API to *Model Plugins*, loading the models at runtime. The *Model Plugins* are precompiled, and therefore no compilation at runtime is necessary. The interface between x-config and the plugins eliminates dynamic loading compatibility issues.

- **Versioning and Migration:** All the models loaded into x-config are versioned, and the process of updating those models triggers the migration of persistent state from one version of the data model to another. The migration mechanism supports simultaneous operation of multiple versions.

- **Synchronization:** It is expected that the backend components being controlled by x-config will periodically fail and restart. Since x-config is the runtime source-of-truth for those components, it takes responsibility for ensuring that they re-synchronize with the latest state upon restart. x-config is able to detect a restart (and trigger the synchronization) because its models include variables that reflect the operational state of those components.

Two points require further elaboration. First, because Atomix is fault-tolerant as long as it runs on multiple physical servers, it can be built on top of unreliable local (per-server) storage. There is no reason to use highly available cloud storage. On the other hand, prudence dictates that all the state the Runtime Control subsystem maintains be backed up periodically, in case it needs to be restarted from scratch due to a catastrophic failure. These checkpoints, plus all the configuration-as-code files stored in a Git repository, collectively define the entirety of the authoritative state needed to (re-)instantiate a cloud deployment.

Second, the set of model definitions are like any other piece of configuration-as-code. They are checked into the code repository and versioned, just as described in Section 4.5. Moreover, the Helm chart that specifies how to deploy the Runtime Control subsystem identifies the version of the models that are to be loaded, analogous to the way Helm charts already identify the version of each microservice (Docker Image) to be deployed. This means the version of the Runtime Control Helm chart effectively specifies the version of the Runtime Control API, since that API is auto-generated from the set of models, as we'll see in the next subsection. All of this is to say that version control for the Northbound Interface of the cloud, as an aggregated whole, is managed in exactly the same way as version control for each functional building block that contributes to the cloud's internal implementation.

5.2.2 Runtime Control API

An API provides an *interface wrapper* that sits between x-config and higher-layer portals and applications. Northbound, it offers a RESTful API. Southbound, it speaks gNMI to x-config. The Runtime Control API layer serves three main purposes:

- Unlike gNMI (which supports only **GET** and **SET** operations), a RESTful API (which supports **GET**, **PUT**, **POST**, **PATCH**, and **DELETE** operations) is expected for GUI development.

- The API layer is an opportunity to implement early parameter validation and security checks. This makes it possible to catch errors closer to the user, and generate more meaningful error messages than is possible with gNMI.

- The API layer defines a "gate" that can be used to audit the history of who performs what operation when (also taking advantage of the identity management mechanism described next).

It is possible to auto-generate the REST API from the set of models loaded into x-config, although one is also free to augment this set with additional "hand-crafted" calls for the sake of convenience (with the caveat that this will likely mean the API is no longer RESTful). The idea of using the model specification as a single source of truth and deriving other artifacts, such as the API, from this specification is appealing because it improves developer productivity, and provides fewer opportunities for inconsistencies to be introduced between layers. Consider, for example, if the developer wishes to add a single field to a model. Without auto-generation, the following must all be updated:

- Model

- API specification

- Stubs that service the API by operating on the models

- Client-side libraries or developer kits

- GUI views that visualize the models

The Aether solution is to use a tool called oapi-codegen to convert the YANG declarations into an OpenAPI3 specification, and then a tool called oapi-codegen to auto-generate the stubs that implement the API.

Auto-generating the API is not without its pitfalls. The models and the API quickly develop a 1:1 correspondence, meaning any change in the modeling is immediately realized as visible change in the API. This means modeling changes must be approached carefully if backward-compatibility is to be preserved. Migration is also more difficult since a single API cannot easily satisfy two sets of models.

An alternative would be to introduce a second external-facing API, and a small translation layer between the auto-generated internal API and the external API. The shim layer would function as a shock absorber, mitigating the frequent bumps that might occur in the internal API. Of course, this presumes the external-facing API is relatively stable, which is problematic if the reason the models are changing in the first place is that the service definition is not yet mature. If the models

Further Reading:
OpenAPI 3.0 (https://swagger.io/specification/).

are changing due to volatility in the backend systems they control, then it is often the case that the models can be distinguished as "low-level" or "high-level", with only the latter directly visible to clients via the API. In semantic versioning terms, a change to a low-level model would then effectively be a backward-compatible PATCH.

5.2.3 Identity Management

Runtime Control leverages an external identity database (an LDAP server) to store user data such as account names and passwords for users who are able to log in. This LDAP server also has the capability to associate users with groups. For example, adding administrators to the AetherAdmin group would be an obvious way to grant those individuals with administrative privileges within Runtime Control.

An external authentication service, Keycloak, serves as a frontend to a database such as LDAP. It authenticates the user, handles the mechanics of accepting the password, validating it, and securely returning the group the user belongs to.

Further Reading:
Keycloak (https://www.keycloak.org/).

The group identifier is then used to grant access to resources within Runtime Control, which points to the related problem of establishing which classes of users are allowed to create/read/write/delete various collections of objects. Like identity management, defining such RBAC policies is well understood, and supported by open source tools. In the case of Aether, Open Policy Agent (OPA) serves this role.

Further Reading:
Policy-based Control (https://www.openpolicyagent.org/).

5.2.4 Adaptors

Not every service or subsystem beneath Runtime Control supports gNMI, and in the case where it is not supported, an adaptor is written to translate between gNMI and the service's native API. In Aether, for example, a gNMI → REST adaptor translates between the Runtime Control's southbound gNMI calls and the SD-Core subsystem's RESTful northbound interface. The adaptor is not necessarily just a syntactic translator, but may also include its own semantic layer. This supports a logical decoupling of the models stored in x-config and the interface used by the southbound device/service, allowing the southbound device/service and Runtime Control to evolve independently.

It also allows for southbound devices/services to be replaced without affecting the northbound interface.

An adaptor does not necessarily support only a single service. An adaptor is one means of taking an abstraction that spans multiple services and applying it to each of those services. An example is the *User Plane Function* (the main packet-forwarding module in the SD-Core User Plane) and *SD-Core*, which are jointly responsible for enforcing *Quality of Service*, where the adaptor applies a single set of models to both services. Care is needed to deal with partial failure, where one service accepts the change but the other does not. In this case, the adaptor keeps trying the failed backend service until it succeeds.

5.2.5 Workflow Engine

The workflow engine, to the left of the x-config in Figure 22, is where multi-step workflows are implemented. For example, defining a new 5G connection or associating devices with an existing connection is a multi-step process, using several models and impacting multiple backend subsystems. In our experience, there may even be complex state machines that implement those steps.

There are well-known open source workflow engines (e.g., Airflow), but our experience is that they do not match up with the types of workflows typical of systems like Aether. As a consequence, the current implementation is ad hoc, with imperative code watching a target set of models and taking appropriate action whenever they change. Defining a more rigorous approach to workflows is a subject of ongoing development.

5.2.6 Secure Communication

gNMI naturally lends itself to mutual TLS for authentication, and that is the recommended way to secure communications between components that speak gNMI. For example, communication between x-config and its adaptors uses gNMI, and therefore, uses mutual TLS. Distributing certificates between components is a problem outside the scope of Runtime Control. It is assumed that another tool will be responsible for distributing, revoking, and renewing certificates.

For components that speak REST, HTTPS is used to secure the connection, and authentication can take place using mechanisms within the HTTPS protocol (basic auth, tokens, etc). Oauth2 and OpenID Connect are leveraged as an authorization provider when using these REST APIs.

5.3 Modeling Connectivity Service

This section sketches the data model for Aether's connectivity service as a way of illustrating the role Runtime Control plays. These models are specified in YANG (for which we include a concrete example of one of the models), but since the Runtime Control API is generated from these specs, it is equally valid to think in terms of an API that supports REST's GET, POST, PUT, PATCH, and DELETE operations on a set of web resources (objects):

- GET: Retrieve an object.

- POST: Create an object.

- PUT, PATCH: Modify an existing object.

- DELETE: Delete an object.

Each object is an instance of one of the YANG-defined models, where every object contains an id field that is used to identify the object. These identifiers are model-specific, so for example, a site has a site-id and an enterprise has an enterprise-id. The models are generally nested, so for example, a site is a member of an enterprise. Objects can also contain references to other objects; such references are implemented using the object's unique id. In a database setting these are often called *foreign keys*.

In addition to the id field, several other fields are also common to all models. These include:

- description: A human-readable description, used to store additional context about the object.

- display-name: A human-readable name that is shown in the GUI.

As these fields are common to all models, we omit them from the per-model descriptions that follow. In the following, we use upper case to denote a model (e.g., Enterprise) and lower case to denote a field within a model (e.g., enterprise).

5.3.1 Enterprises

Aether is deployed in enterprises, and so defines a representative set of organizational abstractions. These include Enterprise, which forms the root of a customer-specific hierarchy. The Enterprise model is the parent of many other objects, and allows those objects to be scoped to a particular Enterprise for ownership and role-based access control purposes. The Enterprise model contains the following field:

- connectivity-service: A list of backend subsystems that implement connectivity for this enterprise. Corresponds to an API endpoint to the SD-Core, SD-Fabric, and SD-RAN.

Enterprises are further divided into Sites. A site is a point-of-presence for an Enterprise and may be either physical or logical (i.e., a single geographic location could contain several logical sites). The Site model contains the following fields:

- imsi-definition: A description of how IMSIs are constructed for this site. Contains the following sub-fields:

  - mcc: Mobile country code.
  - mnc: Mobile network code.
  - enterprise: A numeric enterprise id.
  - format: A mask that allows the above three fields to be embedded into an IMSI. For example CCCNNNEEESSSSSS will construct IMSIs using a 3-digit MCC, 3-digit MNC, 3-digit ENT, and a 6-digit subscriber.

- small-cell: A list of 5G gNodeBs or Access Points or Radios. Each small cell has the following:

  - small-cell-id: Identifier for the small cell. Serves the same purpose as other id fields.

- address: Hostname of the small cell.

- tac: Type Allocation Code.

- enable: If set to true, the small cell is enabled. Otherwise, it is disabled.

The imsi-definition is specific to the mobile cellular network, and corresponds to the unique identifier burned into every SIM card.

5.3.2 *Slices*

Aether models 5G connectivity as a Slice, which represents an isolated communication channel (and associated QoS parameters) that connects a set of devices (modeled as a Device-Group) to a set of applications (each of which is modeled as an Application). Each slice is nested within some site (which is in turn nested inside some enterprise), where for example, an enterprise might configure one slice to carry IoT traffic and another slice to carry video traffic. The Slice model has the following fields:

- device-group: A list of Device-Group objects that can participate in this Slice. Each entry in the list contains both the reference to the Device-Group as well as an enable field which may be used to temporarily remove access to the group.

- app-list: A list of Application objects that are either allowed or denied for this Slice. Each entry in the list contains both a reference to the Application as well as an allow field which can be set to true to allow the application or false to deny it.

- template: Reference to the Template that was used to initialize this Slice.

- upf: Reference to the User Plane Function (UPF) that should be used to process packets for this Slice. It's permitted for multiple Slices to share a single UPF.

- sst, sd: 3GPP-defined slice identifiers assigned by the operations team.

- mbr.uplink, mbr.downlink, mbr.uplink-burst-size, mbr.downlink-burst-size: Aggregate maximum bit-rate and burst sizes of all devices for this slice.

The rate-related parameters are initialized using a selected template, as described below. Also note that this example illustrates how modeling can be used to enforce invariants, in this case, that the Site of the UPF and Device-Group must match the Site of the Slice. That is, the physical devices that connect to a slice and the UPF that implements the core segment of the slice must be constrained to a single physical location.

At one end of a Slice is a Device-Group, which identifies a set of devices that are allowed to use the Slice to connect to various applications. The Device-Group model contains the following fields:

- devices: A list of Devices. Each device has an enable field which can be used to enable or disable the device.

- ip-domain: Reference to an IP-Domain object that describes the IP and DNS settings for UEs within this group.

- mbr.uplink, mbr.downlink: Per-device maximum bit-rate for the device group.

- traffic-class: The traffic class to be used for devices in this group.

At the other end of a Slice is a list of Application objects, which specifies the endpoints for the program devices talk to. The Application model contains the following fields:

- address: The DNS name or IP address of the endpoint.

- endpoint: A list of endpoints. Each has the following fields:

    - name: Name of the endpoint. Used as a key.
    - port-start: Starting port number.
    - port-end: Ending port number.
    - protocol: Protocol (TCP|UDP) for the endpoint.
    - mbr.uplink, mbr.downlink: Per-device maximum bitrate for the application endpoint.

– traffic-class: Traffic class for devices communicating with this application.

Anyone familiar with 3GPP will recognize Aether's Slice abstraction as similar to the specification's notion of a network slice. The Slice model definition includes a combination of 3GPP-specified identifiers (e.g., sst and sd), and details about the underlying implementation (e.g., upf denotes the UPF implementation for the Core's user plane). Although not yet part of the production system, there is a version of Slice that also includes fields related to RAN slicing, with the Runtime Control subsystem responsible for stitching together end-to-end connectivity across the RAN, Core, and Fabric.

An API for Platform Services

We are using Connectivity-as-a-Service as an illustrative example of the role Runtime Control plays, but APIs can be defined for other platform services using the same machinery. For example, because the SD-Fabric in Aether is implemented with programmable switching hardware, the forwarding plane is instrumented with Inband Network Telemetry (INT). A northbound API then enables fine-grained data collection on a per-flow basis, at runtime, making it possible to write closed-loop control applications on top of Aether.

In a similar spirit, the QoS-related control example given in this section could be augmented with additional objects that provide visibility into, and an opportunity to exert control over, various radio-related parameters implemented by SD-RAN. Doing so would be a step towards a platform API that enables a new class of industry automation edge cloud apps.

In general, IaaS and PaaS offerings need to support application- and user-facing APIs that go beyond the DevOps-level configuration files consumed by the underlying software components (i.e., microservices). Creating these interfaces is an exercise in defining a meaningful abstraction layer, which, when done using declarative tooling, becomes an exercise in defining high-level data models. Runtime Control is the management subsystem responsible for specifying and implementing the API for such an abstraction layer.

5.3.3 Templates and Traffic Classes

Associated with each Slice is a QoS-related profile that governs how traffic that slice carries is to be treated. This starts with a Template model, which defines the valid (accepted) connectivity settings. The Aether operations team is responsible for defining these (the features they offer must be supported by the backend subsystems), with enterprises selecting the template they want applied to any instances of the connectivity service they create (e.g., via a drop-down menu). That is, templates are used to initialize Slice objects. The Template model has the following fields:

- sst, sd: Slice identifiers, as specified by 3GPP.

- mbr.uplink, mbr.downlink: Maximum uplink and downlink bandwidth.

- mbr.uplink-burst-size, mbr.downlink-burst-size: Maximum burst size.

- traffic-class: Link to a Traffic-Class object that describes the type of traffic.

Notice that the Device-Group and Application models include similar fields. The idea is that QoS parameters are established for the slice as a whole (based on the selected template) and then individual devices and applications connected to that slice can be assigned their own, more-restrictive QoS parameters on an instance-by-instance basis.

As noted in the previous section, Aether decouples the abstract Slice objects from the implementation details about the backend segments of the end-to-end slices. One reason for this decoupling is that it supports the option of spinning up an entirely new copy of the SD-Core rather than sharing an existing UPF with another Slice. This is done to ensure isolation, and illustrates one possible touch-point between Runtime Control and the Lifecycle Management subsystem: Runtime Control, via an Adaptor, engages Lifecycle Management to launch the necessary set of Kubernetes containers that implement an isolated slice.

The Traffic-Class model specifies the classes of traffic, and includes the following fields:

- arp: Allocation and retention priority.

- qci: QoS class identifier.

- pelr: Packet error loss rate.

- pdb: Packet delay budget.

For completeness, the following shows the corresponding YANG for the Template model. The example omits some introductory boiler-plate for the sake of brevity. The example highlights the nested nature of the model declarations, with both container and leaf fields.

```
module onf-template {
  ...
  description
    "The aether vcs-template holds common parameters used
     by a virtual connectivity service. Templates are used to
     populate a VCS.";
  typedef template-id {
      type yg:yang-identifier {
          length 1..32;
      }
  }
  container template {
    description "The top level container";
    list template {
      key "id";
      description
        "List of vcs templates";
      leaf id {
        type template-id;
        description "ID for this vcs template.";
      }
      leaf display-name {
        type string {
            length 1..80;
        }
        description "display name to use in GUI or CLI";
      }
      leaf sst {
        type at:sst;
        description "Slice/Service type";
```

```
      }
      leaf sd {
        type at:sd;
        description "Slice differentiator";
      }
      container device {
        description "Per-device QOS Settings";
        container mbr {
          description "Maximum bitrate";
          leaf uplink {
            type at:bitrate;
            units bps;
            description "Per-device uplink data rate in mbps";
          }
          leaf downlink {
            type at:bitrate;
            units bps;
            description "Per-device downlink data rate in mbps";
          }
        }
      }
      container slice {
        description "Per-Slice QOS Settings";
        container mbr {
          description "Maximum bitrate";
          leaf uplink {
            type at:bitrate;
            units bps;
            description "Per-Slice mbr uplink data rate in mbps";
          }
          leaf downlink {
            type at:bitrate;
            units bps;
            description "Per-Slice mbr downlink data rate in mbps";
          }
        }
      }
      leaf traffic-class {
        type leafref {
          path "/tc:traffic-class/tc:traffic-class/tc:id";
        }
```

```
        description
          "Link to traffic class";
      }
      leaf description {
        type at:description;
        description "description of this vcs template";
      }
    }
  }
}
```

5.3.4 Other Models

The above description references other models, which we do not fully
describe here. They include IP-Domain, which specifies IP and DNS
settings; and UPF, which specifies the User Plane Function (the data
plane element of the SD-Core) that should forward packets on behalf
of this particular instance of the connectivity service. The UPF model
is necessary because an Aether deployment can run many UPF instances. This is because there are two different implementations (one
runs as a microservice on a server and the other runs as a P4 program
loaded into the switching fabric), and because multiple microservice-
based UPFs can be instantiated at any given time, each isolating a
distinct traffic flow.

5.4 Revisiting GitOps

As we did at the end of Chapter 4, it is instructive to revisit the question of how to distinguish between configuration state and control
state, with Lifecycle Management (and its Config Repo) responsible
for the former, and Runtime Control (and its key-value store) responsible for the latter. Now that we have seen the Runtime Control subsystem in more detail, it is clear that one critical factor is whether or
not a programmatic interface (coupled with an access control mechanism) is required for accessing and changing that state.

Cloud operators and DevOps teams are perfectly capable of checking configuration changes into a Config Repo, which makes it tempt-

Further Reading:
L. Peterson, *et al.* Software-
Defined Networks: A Systems
Approach. November. 2021.

ing to view all state that *could* be specified in a configuration file as Lifecycle-managed configuration state. The availability of enhanced configuration mechanisms, such as Kubernetes *Operators*, make that temptation even greater. But any state that might be touched by someone other than an operator—including enterprise admins and runtime control applications—needs to be accessed via a well-defined API. Giving enterprises the ability to set QoS parameters is an illustrative example. Auto-generating that API from a set of models is an attractive approach to realizing such a control interface, if for no other reason than it forces a decoupling of the interface definition from the underlying implementation (with Adaptors bridging the gap).

UX Considerations

Runtime control touches an important, but often under-appreciated aspect of operating a cloud: taking User Experience (UX) into account. If the only users you're concerned about are the developers and operators of the cloud and its services, who we can assume are comfortable editing a handful of YAML files to execute a change request, then maybe we can stop there. But if we expect end-users to have some ability to steer the system we're building, we also need to "plumb" the low-level variables we've implemented through to a set of dials and knobs that those users can access.

UX Design is a well-established discipline. It is in part about designing GUIs with intuitive workflows, but a GUI depends on a programmatic interface. Defining that interface is the touchpoint between the management and control platform we're focused on in this book, and the users we want to support. This is largely an exercise in defining abstractions, which brings us back to the central point we are trying to make: it is both the reality of the underlying implementation and the mental model of the target users that shape these abstractions. Considering one without the other, as anyone who has read a user's manual understands, is a recipe for disaster.

On this latter point, it is easy to imagine an implementation of a runtime control operation that involves checking a configuration change into the Config Repo and triggering a redeployment. Whether you view such an approach as elegant or clunky is a matter of taste, but how such engineering decisions are resolved depends in large part on how the backend components are implemented. For example, if a configuration change requires a container restart, then there may be little choice. But ideally, microservices are implemented with their own well-defined management interfaces, which can be invoked from either a configuration-time Operator (to initialize the component at boot time) or a control-time Adaptor (to change the component at runtime).

For resource-related operations, such as spinning up additional containers in response to a user request to create a *Slice* or activate an edge service, a similar implementation strategy is feasible. The Kubernetes API can be called from either Helm (to initialize a microservice at boot time) or from a Runtime Control Adaptor (to add resources at runtime). The remaining challenge is deciding which subsystem maintains the authoritative copy of that state, and ensuring that decision is enforced as a system invariant.[13] Such decisions are often situation-dependent, but our experience is that using Runtime Control as the single source-of-truth is a sound approach.

Of course there are two sides to this coin. It is also tempting to provide runtime control of configuration parameters that, at the end of the day, only cloud operators need to be able to change. Configuring the RBAC (e.g., adding groups and defining what objects a given group is allowed to access) is an illustrative example. Unless there is a compelling reason to open such configuration decisions to end users, keeping RBAC-related configuration state (i.e., OPA spec files) in the Config Repo, under the purview of Lifecycle Management, makes complete sense.

These examples illustrate the central value proposition of the runtime control interface, which is to scale operations. It does this by enabling end users and closed-loop control programs to directly steer the system without requiring that the ops team serve as an intermediary.

[13] It is also possible to maintain two authoritative copies of the state, and implement a mechanism to keep them in sync. The difficulty with such a strategy is avoiding back-door access that bypasses the synchronization mechanism.

Chapter 6: Monitoring and Telemetry

Collecting telemetry data for a running system is an essential function of the management platform. It enables operators to monitor system behavior, evaluate performance, make informed provisioning decisions, respond to failures, identify attacks, and diagnose problems. This chapter focuses on three types of telemetry data—*metrics*, *logs*, and *traces*—along with exemplar open source software stacks available to help collect, store, and act upon each of them.

Metrics are quantitative data about a system. These include common performance metrics such as link bandwidth, CPU utilization, and memory usage, but also binary results corresponding to "up" and "down", as well as other state variables that can be encoded numerically. These values are produced and collected periodically (e.g., every few seconds), either by reading a counter, or by executing a runtime test that returns a value. These metrics can be associated with physical resources such as servers and switches, virtual resources such as VMs and containers, or high-level abstractions such as the *Connectivity Service* described in Section 5.3. Given these many possible sources of data, the job of the metrics monitoring stack is to collect, archive, visualize, and optionally analyze this data.

Logs are the qualitative data that is generated whenever a noteworthy event occurs. This information can be used to identify problematic operating conditions (i.e., it may trigger an alert), but more commonly, it is used to troubleshoot problems after they have been detected. Various system components—all the way from the low-level OS kernel to high-level cloud services—write messages that adhere to a well-defined format to the log. These messages include a timestamp, which makes it possible for the logging stack to parse and correlate messages from different components.

Traces are a record of causal relationships (e.g., Service A calls Service B) resulting from user-initiated transactions or jobs. They are related to logs, but provide more specialized information about the context in which different events happen. Tracing is well-understood in a single program, where an execution trace is commonly recorded as an in-memory call stack, but traces are inherently distributed across a graph of network-connected microservices in a cloud setting. This makes the problem challenging, but also critically important because it is often the case that the only way to understand time-dependent phenomena—such as why a particular resource is overloaded—is to understand how multiple independent workflows interact with each other.

Taking a step back from the three types of telemetry data, it is helpful to have a broad understanding of the design space, and to that end, we make four observations.

First, there are two general use cases for telemetry data, which we broadly characterize as "monitoring" and "troubleshooting". We use these terms in the most general way to represent (a) proactively watching for warning signs of trouble (attacks, bugs, failures, overload conditions) in a steady-state system; versus (b) reactively taking a closer look to determine the root cause and resolve an issue (fix a bug, optimize performance, provision more resources, defend against an attack), once alerted to a potential problem. This distinction is important because the former (monitoring) needs to incur minimal overhead and require minimal human involvement, while the latter (troubleshooting) can be more invasive/expensive and typically involves some level of human expertise. This is not a perfect distinction, with plenty of operator activity happening in a gray area, but being aware of the cost/benefit trade-offs of the available tools is an important starting point.

Second, the more aspects of monitoring and troubleshooting that can be automated, the better. This starts with alerts that automatically detect potential problems; typically includes dashboards that make it easy for humans to see patterns and drill down for relevant details across all three types of data; increasingly leverages Machine Learning and statistical analysis to identify deeper connections that are not obvious to human operators; and ultimately supports closed-loop control where the automated tool not only detects problems but is also able to issue corrective control directives. For the purpose of this chapter, we give examples of the first two (alerts and dashboards), and declare the latter two (analytics and close-loop control) as out of scope (but likely running as applications that consume the telemetry data outlined in the sections that follow).

Third, when viewed from the perspective of lifecycle management, monitoring and troubleshooting are just a continuation of testing, except under production workloads rather than test workloads. In fact, the same set of tools can be used on either side of the development-vs-production boundary. For example, as anyone who has profiled a program will recognize and appreciate, tracing is an extremely valuable tool during development—both to track down bugs and to tune performance. Similarly, artificial end-to-end tests can provide value in production systems by triggering early warning alerts. This can be especially helpful when dealing with problematic failure modes.

Finally, because the metrics, logs, and traces collected by the various subsystems are timestamped, it is possible to establish correlations among them, which is helpful when debugging a problem or deciding whether or not an alert is warranted. We give examples of how such telemetry-wide functions are implemented in practice today, and discuss the future of generating and using telemetry data, in the final two sections of this chapter.

6.1 Metrics and Alerts

Starting with metrics, a popular open source monitoring stack uses Prometheus to collect and store platform and service metrics, Grafana to visualize metrics over time, and Alertmanager to notify the operations team of events that require attention. In Aether, Prometheus and Alertmanager are instantiated on each edge cluster, with a single instantiation of Grafana running centrally in the cloud. More information about each tool is available online, so we focus more narrowly on

(1) how individual Aether components "opt into" this stack, and (2) how the stack can be customized in service-specific ways.

Further Reading:
Prometheus (`https://prometheus.io/docs/introduction/overview/`).

Grafana (`https://grafana.com/docs/grafana/latest/getting-started/`).

Alertmanager (`https://prometheus.io/docs/alerting/latest/alertmanager/`).

6.1.1 Exporting Metrics

Individual components implement a *Prometheus Exporter* to provide the current value of the component's metrics. A component's Exporter is queried via HTTP, with the corresponding metrics returned using a simple text format. Prometheus periodically scrapes the Exporter's HTTP endpoint and stores the metrics in its Time Series Database (TSDB) for querying and analysis. Many client libraries are available for instrumenting code to produce metrics in Prometheus format. If a component's metrics are available in some other format, tools are often available to convert the metrics into Prometheus format and export them.

A YAML configuration file specifies the set of Exporter endpoints that Prometheus is to pull metrics from, along will the polling frequency for each endpoint. Alternatively, Kubernetes-based microservices can be extended with a *Service Monitor* Custom Resource Descriptor (CRD) that Prometheus then queries to learn about any Exporter endpoints the microservice has made available.

In addition to component-based Exporters, every edge cluster periodically tests end-to-end connectivity (for various definitions of end-to-end). One test determines whether the 5G control plane is working (i.e., the edge site can reach the SD-Core running in the central cloud) and a second test determines whether the 5G user plane is working (i.e., UEs can reach the Internet). This is a common pattern: individual components can export accumulators and other local variables, but only a "third-party observer" can actively test external behavior, and report the results. These examples correspond to the rightmost "End-to-End Tests" shown in Figure 19 of Chapter 4.

Finally, when a system is running across multiple edge sites, as is the case with Aether, there is an design question of whether monitoring data is stored on the edge sites and lazily pulled to the central location only when needed, or is proactively pushed to the central location as soon as it's generated. Aether employs both approaches, depending on the volume and urgency of the data being collected. By default, metrics collected by the local instantiation of Prometheus stay on the edge sites, and only query results are returned to the central location (e.g., to be displayed by Grafana as described in the next subsection). This is appropriate for metrics that are both high-volume and seldom viewed. One exception is the end-to-end tests described in the previous paragraph. These results are immediately pushed to the central site (bypassing the local Prometheus instance), because they are low-volume and may require immediate attention.

6.1.2 Creating Dashboards

The metrics collected by Prometheus are visualized using Grafana dashboards. In Aether, this means the Grafana instance running as part of AMP in the central cloud sends queries to some combination of the central Prometheus instance and a subset of the Prometheus instances running on edge clusters. For example, Figure 25 shows the summary dashboard for a collection of Aether edge sites.

Figure 25: Central dashboard showing status of Aether edge deployments.

Grafana comes with a set of predefined dashboards for the most common set of metrics—in particular, those associated with physical servers and virtual resources such as containers—but it can also be customized to include dashboards for service-level metrics and other deployment-specific information (e.g., per-enterprise in Aether). For example, Figure 26 shows a custom dashboard for UPF (User Plane Function), the data plane packet forwarder of the SD-Core. The example shows latency and jitter metrics over the last hour at one site, with three additional collapsed panels (PFCP Sessions and Messages) at the bottom.

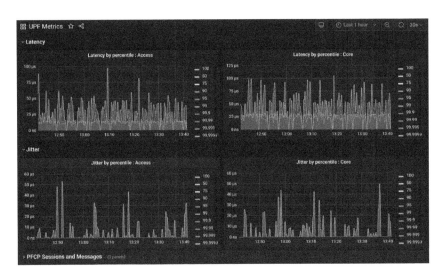

Figure 26: Custom dashboard showing latency and jitter metrics for UPF, the packet forwarding data plane of the SD-Core component.

Briefly, a dashboard is constructed from a set of *panels*, where each panel has a well-defined *type* (e.g., graph, table, gauge, heatmap) bound to a particular Prometheus *query*. New dashboards are created using the Grafana GUI, and the resulting configuration then saved in a JSON file. This configuration file is then committed to the Config Repo, and later loaded into Grafana whenever it is restarted as part of Lifecycle Management. For example, the following code snippet shows the Prometheus query corresponding to the Uptime panel in Figure 25.

```
"expr": "avg(avg_over_time(ace_e2e{endpoint=\"metrics80\",name=\"$edge\"}[$__interval]) * 100)"
```

Note that this expression includes variables for the site ($edge) and the interval over which the uptime is computed ($__interval).

6.1.3 Defining Alerts

Alerts can be triggered in Prometheus when a component metric crosses some threshold. Alertmanager is a tool that then routes the alert to one or more receivers, such as an email address or Slack channel.

An alert for a particular component is defined by an *alerting rule*, an expression involving a Prometheus query, such that whenever it evaluates to true for the indicated time period, it triggers a corresponding message to be routed to a set of receivers. These rules are recorded in a YAML file that is checked into the Config Repo and loaded into Prometheus. (Alternatively, Helm Charts for individual components can define rules via *Prometheus Rule* custom resources.) For example, the following code snippet shows the Prometheus Rule for two alerts, where the expr lines corresponds to the respective queries submitted to Prometheus.

```
- alert: SingleEdgeTestNotReporting
  annotations:
    message: |
      Cluster {{'{{ .Labels.name }}'}} has not reported for at least 5 minutes.
  expr: (time() - aetheredge_last_update{endpoint="metrics80"}) > 300
  for: 1m
  labels:
    severity: critical
- alert: SingleEdgeConnectTestFailing
  annotations:
    message: |
      Cluster {{'{{ .Labels.name }}'}} reporting UE connect failure for at least 10 minutes.
  expr: aetheredge_connect_test_ok{endpoint="metrics80"} < 1
  for: 10m
  labels:
    severity: critical
```

In Aether, the Alertmanager is configured to send alerts with *critical* or *warning* severity to a general set of receivers. If it is desirable to route a specific alert to a different receiver (e.g., a Slack channel used by the developers for that particular component), the Alertmanager configuration is changed accordingly.

6.2 Logging

OS programmers have been writing diagnostic messages to a *syslog* since the earliest days of Unix. Originally collected in a local file, the syslog abstraction has been adapted to cloud environments by adding a suite of scalable services. Today, one typical open source logging stack uses Fluentd to collect (aggregate, buffer, and route) log messages written by a set of components, with Fluentbit serving as a client-side agent running in each component helping developers normalize their log messages. ElasticSearch is then used to store, search, and analyze those messages, with Kibana used to display and visualize the results. The general flow of data is shown in Figure 27, using the main Aether subsystems as illustrative sources of log messages.

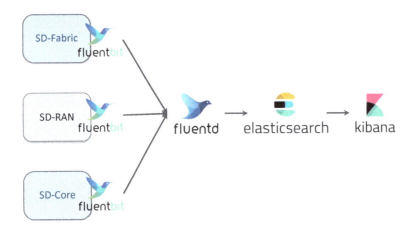

Figure 27: Flow of log messages through the Logging subsystem.

Further Reading:
Fluentd (https://docs.fluentd.org/).

ElasticSearch (https://www.elastic.co/elasticsearch/).

Kibana (https://www.elastic.co/kibana/).

6.2.1 Common Schema

The key challenge in logging is to adopt a uniform message format across all components, a requirement that is complicated by the fact that the various components integrated in a complex system are often developed independently of each other. Fluentbit plays a role in normalizing these messages by supporting a set of filters. These filters parse "raw" log messages written by the component (an ASCII string), and output "canonical" log messages as structured JSON. There are other options, but JSON is reasonably readable as text, which still matters for debugging by humans. It is also well-supported by tooling.

For example, developers for the SD-Fabric component might write a log message that looks like this:

```
2020-08-18 05:35:54.842Z INFO [DistributedP4RuntimeTableMirror] Synchronized TABLE_ENTRY \
mirror for device:leaf1: 0 removed, 2 updated, 4 added
```

where a Fluentbit filter transforms into a structure that looks like this:

```
{
    "time": "2020-08-18 05:35:54.842Z",
    "logLevel": "INFO",  "component": "DistributedP4RuntimeTableMirror",
    "log": "Synchronized TABLE_ENTRY mirror for device:leaf1: 0 removed, 2 updated, 4 added"
}
```

This example is simplified, but it does serve to illustrate the basic idea. It also highlights the challenge the DevOps team faces in building the management platform, which is to decide on a meaningful set of name/value pairs for the system as a whole. In other words, they must define a common schema for these structured log messages. The *Elastic Common Schema* is a good place to start that definition, but among other things, it will be necessary to establish the accepted set of log levels, and conventions for using each level. In Aether, for example, the log levels are: FATAL, ERROR, WARNING, INFO, and DEBUG.

6.2.2 Best Practices

Establishing a shared logging platform is, of course, of little value unless all the individual components are properly instrumented to write log messages. Programming languages typically come with library support for writing log messages (e.g., Java's log4j), but that's just a start. Logging is most effective if the components adhere to the following set of best practices.

- **Log shipping is handled by the platform.** Components should assume that stdout/stderr is ingested into the logging system by

Further Reading:
Elastic Common Schema
(`https://www.elastic.co/guide/en/ecs/current/index.html`).

Fluentbit (or similar tooling), and avoid making the job more complicated by trying to route their own logs. The exception is for external services and hardware devices that are outside the management platform's control. How these systems send their logs to a log aggregator must be established as a part of the deployment process.

- **File logging should be disabled.** Writing log files directly to a container's layered file system is proven to be I/O inefficient and can become a performance bottleneck. It is also generally unnecessary if the logs are also being sent to stdout/stderr. Generally, logging to a file is discouraged when a component runs in a container environment. Instead, components should stream all logs to the collecting system.

- **Asynchronous logging is encouraged.** Synchronous logging can become a performance bottleneck in a scaled environment. Components should write logs asynchronously.

- **Timestamps should be created by the program's logger.** Components should use the selected logging library to create timestamps, with as precise a timestamp as the logging framework allows. Using the shipper or logging handlers may be slower, or create timestamps on receipt, which may be delayed. This makes trying to align events between multiple services after log aggregation problematic.

- **Must be able to change log levels without interrupting service.** Components should provide a mechanism to set the log level at startup, and an API that allows the log level to be changed at runtime. Scoping the log level based on specific subsystems is a useful feature, but not required. When a component is implemented by a suite of microservices, the logging configuration need only be applied to one instance for it to apply to all instances.

6.3 Distributed Tracing

Execution traces are the third source of telemetry data. Tracing is challenging in a cloud setting because it involves following the flow of control for each user-initiated request across multiple microservices. The good news is that instrumenting a set of microservices involves activating tracing support in the underlying language runtime system—typically in the RPC stubs—rather than asking app developers to explicitly instrument their programs.

The general pattern is similar to what we've already seen with metrics and logs: the running code is instrumented to produce data that is then collected, aggregated, stored, and made available for display and analysis. The main difference is the type of data we're interested in collecting, which, for tracing, is typically the sequence of API boundary crossings from one module to another. This data gives us the information we need to reconstruct the call chain. In principle, we could leverage the logging system to support tracing—and just be diligent in logging the necessary interface-crossing information—but it is a specialized enough use case to warrant its own vocabulary, abstractions, and mechanisms.

At a high level, a *trace* is a description of a transaction as it moves through the system. It consists of a sequence of *spans* (each of which represents work done within a service) interleaved with a set of *span contexts* (each of which represents the state carried across the network from one service to another). An illustrative example of a trace is shown in Figure 28, but abstractly, a trace is a directed graph with nodes that correspond to spans and edges that correspond to span contexts. The nodes and edges are then timestamped and annotated with relevant facts (key/value tags) about the end-to-end execution path, including when and for how long it ran. Each span also includes timestamped log messages generated while the span was executing, simplifying the process of correlating log messages with traces.

Again, as with metrics and log messages, the details are important and those details are specified by an agreed-upon data model. The OpenTelemetry project is now defining one such model, building on the earlier OpenTracing project (which was in turn influenced by the Dapper distributed tracing mechanism developed by Google). Beyond the challenge of defining a model that captures the most relevant semantic information, there is the pragmatic issue of (1) minimizing the overhead of tracing so as not to negatively impact application

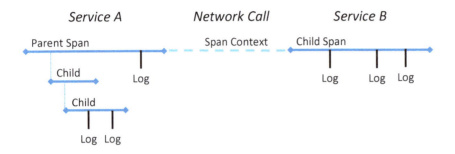

Figure 28: Example trace spanning two network services.

performance, yet (2) extracting enough information from traces so as to make collecting it worthwhile. Sampling is a widely adopted technique introduced into the data collection pipeline to manage this trade-off. One consequence of these challenges is that distributed tracing is the subject of ongoing research, and we can expect the model definitions and sampling techniques to evolve and mature in the foreseeable future.

With respect to mechanisms, Jaeger is a widely used open source tracing tool originally developed by Uber. (Jaeger is not included in Aether, but was utilized in a predecessor edge cloud.) Jaeger includes instrumentation of the runtime system for the language(s) used to implement an application, a collector, storage, and a query language that can be used to diagnose performance problems and do root cause analysis.

Further Reading:

B. Sigelman, *et al.* Dapper, a Large-Scale Distributed Systems Tracing Infrastructure. Google Technical Report. April 2010.

OpenTelemetry (https://opentelemetry.io/).

Jaeger (https://www.jaegertracing.io/).

6.4 Integrated Dashboards

The metrics, logs and traces being generated by instrumented application software make it possible to collect a wealth of data about the health of a system. But this instrumentation is only useful if the right data is displayed to the right people (those with the ability to take action) at the right time (when action needs to be taken). Creating useful panels and organizing them into intuitive dashboards is part of the solution, but integrating information across the subsystems of the management platform is also a requirement.

Unifying all this data is the ultimate objective of ongoing efforts like the OpenTelemetry project mentioned in the previous section, but there are also opportunities to use the tools described in this chapter to better integrate data. This section highlights two general strategies.

First, both Kibana and Grafana can be configured to display telemetry data from multiple sources. For example, it is straightforward to integrate both logs and traces in Kibana. This is typically done by first feeding the tracing data into ElasticSearch, which Kibana then queries. Similarly, it is useful to have a convenient way to see the log messages associated with a particular component in the context of metrics that have been collected. This is easy to accomplish because Grafana can be configured to display data from ElasticSearch just as easily as from Prometheus. Both are data sources that can be queried. This makes it to possible to create a Grafana dashboard that includes a selected set of log messages, similar to the one from Aether shown in Figure 29. In this example, we see INFO-level messages associated with the UPF sub-component of SD-Core, which augments the UPF performance data shown in Figure 26.

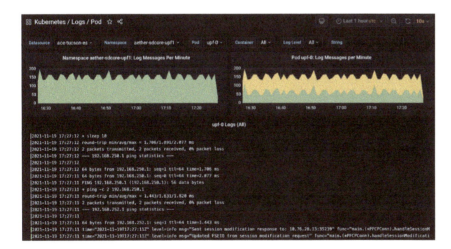

Figure 29: Log messages associated with the UPF element of SD-Core, displayed in a Grafana dashboard.

Second, the runtime control interface described in Chapter 5 provides a means to change various parameters of a running system, but to make informed decisions about what changes (if any) need to be made, it is necessary to have access to the right data. To this end, it is ideal to have access to both the "knobs" and the "dials" on an integrated dashboard. This can be accomplished by incorporating Grafana frames in the Runtime Control GUI, which, in its simplest form, displays a set of web forms corresponding to the fields in the underlying data models. (More sophisticated control panels are certainly possible.)

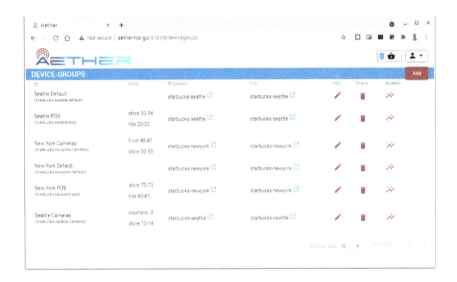

Figure 30: Example control dashboard showing the set of Device Groups defined for a fictional set of Aether sites.

For example, Figure 30 shows the set of device groups for a fictional set of Aether sites, where clicking on the "Edit" button pops up a web form that lets the enterprise admin modify the corresponding fields of the Device-Group model (not shown), and clicking on the "Monitor" button pops up a Grafana-generated frame similar to the one shown in Figure 31. In principle, this frame is tailored to show only the most relevant information associated with the selected object.

6.5 Observability

Knowing what telemetry data to collect, so you have exactly the right information when you need it, but doing so without negatively impacting system performance, is a difficult problem. *Observability* is a relatively new term being used to describe this general problem space, and while the term can be dismissed as the latest marketing buzzword (which it is), it can also be interpreted as another of the set of *"-ities"*

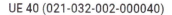

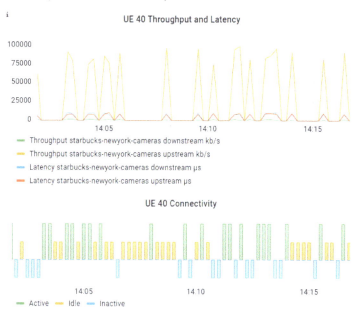

that all good systems aspire to, alongside scalability, reliability, availability, security, usability, and so on. Observability is the quality of a system that makes visible the facts about its internal operation needed to make informed management and control decisions. It has become a fertile space for innovation, and so we conclude this chapter with two examples that may become commonplace in the near future.

The first is *Inband Network Telemetry (INT)*, which takes advantage of programmable switching hardware to allow operators to ask new questions about how packets are being processed "in-band", as they flow through the network. This is in contrast to either depending on the predefined set of counters hardwired into fixed-function network devices, or being able to inspect just a sampled subset of packets. Because Aether uses programmable switches as the foundation for its SDN-based switching fabric, it is able to use INT as a fourth type of telemetry data, and in doing so provide qualitatively deeper insights into traffic patterns and the root causes of network failures.

For example, INT has been used to measure and record queuing delay individual packets experience while traversing a sequence of switches along an end-to-end path, making it possible to detect *microbursts* (queuing delays measured over millisecond or even sub-millisecond time scales). It is even possible to correlate this information across packet flows that followed different routes, so as to determine which flows shared buffer capacity at each switch. As another example, INT has been used to record the decision making process that directed how packets are delivered, that is, which forwarding rules were applied at each switch along the end-to-end path. This opens the door to using INT to verify that the data plane is faithfully executing the forwarding behavior the network operator intends. For more information about INT, we refer the reader to our companion SDN book.

The second is the emergence of *Service Meshes* mentioned in Chapter 1. A Service Mesh framework such as Istio provides a means to enforce fine-grained security policies and collect telemetry data in cloud native applications by injecting "observation/enforcement points" between microservices. These injection points, called *sidecars*, are typically implemented by a container that "runs alongside" the containers that implement each microservice, with all RPC calls from Service A to Service B passing through their associated sidecars. As shown in Figure 32, these sidecars then implement whatever policies the operator wants to impose on the application, sending telemetry data to a global collector and receiving security directives from a global policy engine.

From the perspective of observability, sidecars can be programmed to record whatever information operators might want to collect, and in principle, they can even be dynamically updated as conditions warrant. This provides a general way for operators to define how the system is observed without having to rely on instrumentation developers might include in their services. The downside is that sidecars impose a nontrivial amount of overhead on inter-service communication. For that reason, alternative approaches to sidecars are gaining traction,

Further Reading:
L. Peterson, *et al.* Software-Defined Networking: A Systems Approach. November 2021.

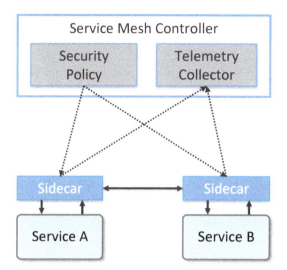

Figure 32: Overview of a Service Mesh framework, with sidecars intercepting messages flowing between Services A and B. Each sidecar enforces security policy received from the central controller and sends telemetry data to the central controller.

notably Cilium, which uses eBPF (extended Berkeley Packet Filters) to implement observability, security and networking data plane features inside the kernel rather than in a sidecar.

For more information about the Istio Service Mesh, we recommend Calcote and Butcher's book. The Cilium project has extensive documentation and tutorials at its web site.

Further Reading:
L. Calcote and Z. Butcher Istio: Up and Running. October 2019.

Cilium: eBPF-based Networking, Observability, Security (`https://cilium.io/`).

About The Book

Source for *Edge Cloud Operations: A Systems Approach* is available on GitHub under terms of the Creative Commons (CC BY-NC-ND 4.0) license. The community is invited to contribute corrections, improvements, updates, and new material under the same terms. While this license does not automatically grant the right to make derivative works, we are keen to discuss derivative works (such as translations) with interested parties. Please reach out to discuss@systemsapproach.org.

If you make use of this work, the attribution should include the following information:

Read the Book

This book is part of the Systems Approach Series, with an online version published at `https://ops.systemsapproach.org`.

To track progress and receive notices about new versions, you can follow the project on Mastodon (`https://discuss.systems/@SystemsAppr`). To read a running commentary on how the Internet is evolving, and for updates on our writing projects, you can sign up for the Systems Approach newsletter (`https://systemsapproach.org/newsletter`).

Build the Book

To build a web-viewable version, you first need to download the source:

```
$ mkdir ~/ops
$ cd ~/ops
$ git clone https://github.com/SystemsApproach/ops.git
```

The build process is stored in the Makefile and requires Python be installed. The Makefile will create a virtualenv (venv-docs) which installs the documentation generation toolset. You may also need to install the enchant C library using your system's package manager for the spelling checker to function properly.

To generate HTML in _build/html, run make html.

To check the formatting of the book, run make lint.

To check spelling, run make spelling. If there are additional words, names, or acronyms that are correctly spelled but not in the dictionary, please add them to the dict.txt file.

To see the other available output formats, run make.

Contribute to the Book

We hope that if you use this material, you are also willing to contribute back to it. If you are new to open source, you might check out the How to Contribute to Open Source guide at https://opensource. guide/how-to-contribute/. Among other things, you'll learn about posting *Issues* that you'd like to see addressed, and issuing *Pull Requests* to merge your improvements back into GitHub.

If you'd like to contribute and are looking for something that needs attention, see the wiki for the current TODO list.

About The Authors

Larry Peterson is the Robert E. Kahn Professor of Computer Science, Emeritus at Princeton University, where he served as Chair from 2003-2009. His research focuses on the design, implementation, and operation of Internet-scale distributed systems, including the widely used PlanetLab and MeasurementLab platforms. He is currently contributing to the Aether access-edge cloud project at the Linux Foundation. Peterson is a member of the National Academy of Engineering, a Fellow of the ACM and the IEEE, the 2010 recipient of the IEEE Kobayashi Computer and Communication Award, and the 2013 recipient of the ACM SIGCOMM Award. He received his Ph.D. degree from Purdue University.

Scott Baker is a Cloud Software Architect at Intel, where he works on the Open Edge Platform. Prior to joining Intel, he was on the Open Networking Foundation (ONF) engineering team that built Aether, leading the runtime control effort. Baker has also worked on cloud-related research projects at Princeton and the University of Arizona, including PlanetLab, GENI, and VICCI. He received his Ph.D. in Computer Science from the University of Arizona in 2005.

Andy Bavier is a Cloud Software Engineer at Intel, where he works on the Open Edge Platform. Prior to joining Intel, he was on the Open Networking Foundation (ONF) engineering team that built Aether, leading the observability effort. Bavier has also been a Research Scientist at Princeton University, where he worked on the PlanetLab project. He received a BA in Philosophy from William & Mary in 1990, an MS in Computer Science from the University of Arizona in 1995, and a PhD in Computer Science from Princeton University in 2004.

Zack Williams is a Cloud Software Engineer at Intel, where he works on the Open Edge Platform. Prior to joining Intel, he was on the Open Networking Foundation (ONF) engineering team that built Aether, leading the infrastructure provisioning effort. Williams has also been a systems programmer at the University of Arizona. He received his BS in Computer Science from the University of Arizona in 2001.

Bruce Davie is a computer scientist noted for his contributions to the field of networking. He began his networking career at Bellcore where he worked on the Aurora Gigabit testbed and collaborated with Larry Peterson on high-speed host-network interfaces. He then went to Cisco where he led a team of architects responsible for Multiprotocol Label Switching (MPLS). He worked extensively at the IETF on standardizing MPLS and various quality of service technologies. He also spent five years as a visiting lecturer at the Massachusetts Institute of Technology. In 2012 he joined Software Defined Networking (SDN) startup Nicira and was then a principal engineer at VMware following the acquisition of Nicira. In 2017 he took on the role of VP and CTO for the Asia Pacific region at VMware. He is a Fellow of the ACM and chaired ACM SIGCOMM from 2009 to 2013. Davie is the author of multiple books and the holder of more than 40 U.S. patents.

www.ingramcontent.com/pod-product-compliance
Lightning Source LLC
Chambersburg PA
CBHW040217090326
40690CB00065B/5285